D0758855

Financing and Managing
Fast-Growth Companies

Financing and Managing Fast-Growth Companies

The Venture Capital Process

George Kozmetsky
Michael D. Gill, Jr.
Raymond W. Smilor
IC² Institute
The University of Texas at Austin

Lexington Books
D.C. Heath and Company/Lexington, Massachusetts/Toronto

"The Role of the Venture Capitalist in the Entrepreneurial Process" by Lucien Ruby is adapted with permission from the book *Corporate Creativity: Robust Companies and the Entrepreneurial Spirit*, edited by Raymond W. Smilor and Robert L. Kuhn © 1984 Praeger Publishers.

Library of Congress Cataloging in Publication Data

Kozmetsky, George.
Financing and managing fast-growth companies

1. Venture capital—United States. 2. Venture capital. I. Gill, Michael D. II. Smilor, Raymond W. III. Title.
HG4963.K69   1985   658.1′52   84-48473
ISBN 0-669-09481-1 (alk. paper)

Published simultaneously in Canada
Printed in the United States of America on acid-free paper
International Standard Book Number: 0-669-09481-1
Library of Congress Catalog Card Number: 84-48473

Contents

List of Figures

List of Tables

Foreword: The Role of the Venture Capitalist in the Entrepreneurial Process

Lucien Ruby

In 1972 I decided to start a company, and I managed to convince some very foolish venture capitalists to put up $750,000. Not a bad amount for 1972! But being from a traditional Southern family that was entrepreneurially oriented, I had to do one thing. I had to go back to Kentucky and talk it over with the patriarch of the family, my Uncle Hooks, who was about 90 years old and had never been in good health. When I got there, Uncle Hooks was in the hospital. He had tubes running in and out, and there were monitors going every which way. I walked in, pulled up a chair right beside him, leaned over, and outlined the deal in his ear. He did not open his eyes. He lay there until I finished the description of what I was going to do. I even gave him the business plan. All of a sudden, he started shaking and he forced himself to sit up. He grabbed me around the shirt collar and said, "Don't let those bloodsuckers near your company!"

Like others, he had the attitude that the venture capitalist community was composed of "vulture" capitalists. Some of this attitude still exists, and I think in certain cases it is rightfully so. While some people have had bad experiences with venture capitalists, many have had good ones. Part of the problem stems from the fact that people do not know who venture capitalists really are or what they do.

Times are very good for venture capitalists right now. There is more money coming into the industry than before. This is due to the successful lobbying effort for reduction of the capital gains tax. It is also due to the removal of impediments to pension funds investing in venture capital pools. As a result, since 1982 pension funds have dumped more money into the venture capital community than existed in the prior two decades.

Lucien Ruby is a practicing venture capitalist. He has been a principal with Brentwood Associates and he is now forming his own venture capital firm specializing in high technology start-ups.

I would like to talk about the basic concepts that drive most professional venture capitalists, discuss what makes for a good deal, and then review the problems that we face.

Queen Isabella is a perfect example of a professional venture capitalist at his or her best. Some crazy entrepreneur showed up and talked to her about another dumb research and development idea. Columbus did not invent the concept that the earth was round. He was working on the "D" part instead of the "R" part. She listened and then asked a lot of people whether they thought it made sense. She called in navigators, the pope, and others, and then flew right in the face of their advice. She hocked the family jewels and proceeded to give funding. If she had stopped there, it would have been the same kind of investing as giving somebody money on Saturday night. But she went further. She gave management assistance by suggesting three ships instead of two, and she used her not-so-insignificant influence in recruiting. The queen also did something else that was quite important and that most people do not think that venture capitalists do: she did not take all the profit. She took a hefty slice because she was taking a risk on a person who was getting ready to sail off the edge of the earth according to all of her best advisors, but she left some for Columbus and his crew. (Of course, the crew also got to survive.)

This is essentially the way that modern, effective, institutional venture capitalists work. There are five guidelines that are vital in a venture capitalist's approach to an investment. (These guidelines were developed by General Georges Doriot who founded the American Research and Development venture pool and who is considered the father of the venture capital industry in the United States.)

1. Don't try to run the business. You don't know how to do it as a venture capitalist; the entrepreneur knows best. Entrepreneurs can't understand this point because they believe the venture capitalist will try to run the company.
2. Treat the portfolio companies, these little companies you have invested in, like your own children. Kick them every now and then if they need it, but be fair.
3. Be a help. Be there when needed. Be an ear, a sounding board, an alter ego, a crying towel.
4. (I think this is the key.) Do what is necessary to allow the portfolio company the opportunity to achieve the potential you originally thought you saw was there. In other words, don't pull the plug too soon. For example, General Doriot practiced that. If he had not followed that dictum, Digital Equipment Corporation would have been shut down during its second year of operation. He kept it going at a bad time and provided manage-

ment help in the form of Ken Olson; his $67,000 investment became worth well over $600 million.

5. Be realistic. Don't get swept away. It is very easy to listen to an entrepreneur and start getting fired up. Entrepreneurs are persuasive people. But a venture capitalist can't let himself lose his objectivity.

Given these guidelines for modern venture capitalists, what is the business beyond the conceptual level? It is well and good to talk about a concept, but a person can drown in a conceptual lagoon if not careful.

What is it that venture capitalists want? It is very simple. We want a very large capital gain and a sane lifestyle. And it is not clear to me that they go together. The large capital gain is driven by greed—simple enough. The sane lifestyle is driven by a desire for quality of life. But how can the two be merged? How can the venture capitalist get involved while letting the entrepreneur be free to do what is necessary to develop the products, processes, and markets that are important? The key is to "do good deals," which is similar to the advice to "buy low, sell high." Both are true enough. The practical problem is to actually do it! In doing deals, one goes through a chronological process: select, structure, monitor, and exit. Select a good deal; structure it so that you get the best possible return that you can; monitor it by giving help when needed and following through; and then get out. Go public or sell it to someone. But get your return and do not be greedy. Chronologically, that is the way it goes. However, in order of importance to the venture capitalist, the activities are:

1. The monitoring process,
2. The selection process,
3. The exit procedure, and
4. The structure of the deal.

The only time the structure of a deal truly matters is when the company heads south—when everybody is scrambling for the exits. Because his partners are suddenly calling on him, the venture capitalist wants to have the structure in a position so that he has preference and can at least escape with something. He will never get out with his pride on one of these deals if it goes under, but he may get out with something. So the entrepreneur need not spend a lot of time talking to the venture capitalists about subordinated debentures or preferred stock warrants since it is not comparatively important. Structure will become an issue, but it is not critical in solidifying the deal done.

Regarding exit, a venture capitalist would like to know how he is going to get out of a deal—how he is going to turn an investment into a capital gain. There is a certain amount of stability given to a company by a public offering, but the timing must be right.

The monitoring process, which I think is the most important factor in a venture capital firm's success, takes the form of providing help when needed. We do a lot of recruiting for our companies. The recruiting process for the vice-president of marketing or finance, for example, is a time-consuming process. We can help the entrepreneur because we have lots of contacts. We also get as many as thirty resumes a week from people who are interested in jobs. By keeping these on file and reviewing them, we help our companies. Planning is another important monitoring area. When entrepreneurs need new funding, we get involved in the treasury process. We will do whatever is necessary to help the company continue, but we will not become a full-time employee or part of the management team unless it is absolutely necessary to assist a troubled company.

The selection process is affected primarily by the entrepreneur. What is a good deal? How do we select a good deal? Ten times your money in five years is a good deal. We look for that. It is easy to look at one that made it and say, "That was a good deal." But how do you find one? How do you predict what is going to happen?

Most venture capitalists and venture capital firms in the United States have a selection process that has extremely rigid guidelines, with an extraordinarily liberal exception policy! For instance, Brentwood is a high technology start-up investor that requires a minimum investment in the range of $750,000 to $1 million. So why did we invest in an airline company, Midway Airlines? Why did we buy out JBL Speakers? Our liberal exception policy! The structure that we put on a required deal has more to do with the characteristics of the people in the industry and the company itself than it does with a particular industry.

For most venture capitalists there has to be the possibility of seeing a ten-times return on invested money in five years. We do not have to get it (because we usually do not), but we want to see that it is possible. There is no point in a venture capitalist's investing in a company that requires sales to be three times bigger than the projected market. The project must be within the realm of reality. Consequently, the market must be big. A big market has a lot of room in it; it can be segmented, and usually there is some part of it that somebody has forgotten. The market must also be growing. A growing market is extraordinarily forgiving. You would not believe the problems that were encountered with Apple Computer in its early stages. The company made lots of mistakes, but the market was so forgiving! People were ripping that computer off the loading dock. It was incredible! The market grew so fast that the management was able to make mistakes and still do well. Part of the reason for this was that the company had a proprietary edge. That edge— be it a technology or a marketing strategy, for example—is a great incentive for a venture capitalist.

Good partners are important in making an investment. There has been a lot of discussion about whether the venture capital community and small business enterprises can live with big companies. Yes, they can, as long as the goals, the aims, the desires, the needs, and the wants of all partners are the same. When they diverge, there is a problem. It is like going to bed with an elephant. Everything is great until the elephant decides it is uncomfortable and wants to roll over. Then the arrangement is difficult at best and dangerous at times.

The most critical part of a new venture is good management. It is also the most subjective. We can find out about the projections for markets, the technology, and whether there is a proprietary edge. The challenge is ascertaining whether the management is good or bad. The only way to do that is to get to know the management personnel very well by spending time with them. Entrepreneurs become tired of venture capitalists because we are always there, always asking questions.

A venture capitalist needs to know the entrepreneur. He needs to know his weaknesses, strengths, pitfalls, blind spots, and biases. Only by knowing the entrepreneur can he identify where the potential problems may be. The reference check is one simple but effective technique. Some fifteen reference checks on everybody in the management team is not unusual.

An entrepreneur needs a team. In fact, a team approach to starting a company makes a lot of sense because an entrepreneur cannot do it all. It is not surprising that the Dun & Bradstreet failure record, which tracks bankruptcies in corporations, indicates that over 90 percent of companies fail because of management shortcomings. A successful entrepreneur needs to have other people with him. The team does not need to be complete at the start because an entrepreneur can put the pieces together after the company is funded. Indeed, the most important person in the start-up of an entrepreneurial company is the vice-president of common sense. Unfortunately, too few companies have one.

What are the problems? Why would a venture capitalist cry? First, even in good times, entrepreneurs are strange birds. They are smart, bright, and sometimes realistic. But right now on my desk there are about twenty business plans claiming that within three years the companies will be bigger than General Motors. So entrepreneurs have blind spots.

Second, the technology is changing very rapidly, perhaps too rapidly. Show me an engineer who has been out of the mainstream of a particular technology for six months, and I will show you a person who is two years behind.

Third, the marketplace in most of these start-up companies is dynamic, easy to misjudge, and constantly changing. No one ever fulfills his plan. In fact, we have never seen anybody make his plan except one person in whom we did not invest. I have a rule that when I make an investment, I tell those in the company to cancel the first board of directors meeting and mail me their updated projections because I know they will have changed.

Fourth, all of us have our limits. Entrepreneurs reach thresholds, companies reach thresholds. The skills that were important when a company began are no longer important as it matures. As a result people have to change or they have to leave. And it is difficult to fire the founder of a company. The difficulty is not walking in and saying, "You are out," but the agonizing reach for that point. If the venture capitalist decides to do it, he is usually late.

With a strong entrepreneur, a good leader, and a good team, all of these threats to my sanity are reduced greatly, and all of the problems associated with my not earning a large capital gain are reduced.

What about the future? The venture capital industry is changing. Super-funds are upon us. Kliner-Perkins is at $150 million, and Welsh-Carson-Anderson & Stowe is at $100 million. Brentwood Associates recently received commitments of $150 million four days before the offering memorandum was put out. They turned away approximately $40 million. That is more money in one fund than went into the entire venture capital community from 1971 to 1975. It is going to be different out there. But the world of venture capitalists is different from the world of entrepreneurs. Venture capitalists are followers. We go where the entrepreneurs are. Entrepreneurs will be in the driver's seat, which, of course, is a good thing.

I anticipate a two-tiered structure to the venture capital industry. Big funds will handle the $2.5 million to $3 million investments, while small funds will do the $50,000 to $100,000 to $150,000 investments (and provide a lot of help). This arrangement is good for the industry, good for the country, good for the venture capital community, and good for the entrepreneur. On the other hand, there is a shortage of venture capital people; this will create frustrations because a lot of money will be available, but will not be dispersed quickly enough.

Venture capitalists will follow the entrepreneur because the entrepreneur, not the venture capitalist, is the key to the whole process. Venture capitalists are an integral part of the entrepreneurial spirit, but they are not the key. With apologies to William Faulkner, the entrepreneur will not simply endure; the entrepreneur will prevail.

Preface

Capital is the catalyst in the entrepreneurial chain reaction. It is the life blood of emerging and expanding enterprises. It is the sine qua non of a new product, an innovative service, or a brilliant idea. Fortunately, a growing pool of capital is being created in the United States today. This capital is being institutionalized and managed by professionals whose business it is to invest in potentially successful growth ventures. Although limited in number, these professionals are forming a coherent and formal venture capital industry. Venture capital is a high-risk, high-stakes business with the promise of great rewards for those who can pick winners.

Capital venturing is the dynamic and creative process by which capital investments in emerging enterprises are made, managed, and developed. This process is risky, particularly for technology-based companies, because of the intense competition in the marketplace, the inherent difficulties associated with start-up companies, and the ever-present potential for miscalculation. Unforeseen changes in the domestic and international marketplaces as well as in regulations make the process even more uncertain.

The entrepreneur is the real driver behind new business development. And perhaps the most significant link between the entrepreneur, especially when he is technologically oriented, and the commercialization of his product or service, is the venture capital industry. This industry provides risk capital and sophisticated managerial assistance to the entrepreneur in return for a piece of the action, thus serving as a conduit between the innovator and the marketplace.

But what is venture capital? Where does it come from? How is it invested? What is the role of venture capitalists in the entrepreneurial process and what do they expect to gain? How are venture capital investments determined? How do venture-backed companies become successful? What impact does the venture capital industry have on a state and a community? What aspects of national policy encourage or inhibit the venture capital industry in fostering economic and business development?

By addressing these issues and others, this book attempts to place venture capital in perspective as an innovative financing strategy whose contribution to the commercialization process includes not only capital, but also expertise, innovative management, and human resources.

Acknowledgments

Completing a book is like succeeding in an entrepreneurial venture. Both involve risk, hard work, and not a little bit of luck. They also require the support and encouragement of talented people and organizations.

Many venture capitalists have been an important source of knowledge and information for us. We especially wish to acknowledge Arthur Rock, E.F. "Ned" Heizer, Gregory A. Kozmetsky, J. Michael Bell, Terry Dorsey, Pat Hamner, Lowell H. Lebermann, Jr., and Lucien Ruby.

We are indebted to many colleagues at the University of Texas at Austin for contributing to our understanding of creative and innovative management and technology venturing. We particularly want to thank Eugene Konecci, Abraham Charnes, W.W. Cooper, Robert Peterson, Kenneth Land, Timothy Ruefli and Robert L. Kuhn. We are also grateful to members of the boards of directors and key management executives of several entrepreneurial companies, including Teledyne, Heizer Corporation, Datapoint, Amdahl, La Quinta, ETA Systems, MCO Resources, Maxxam, and Wrather Corporation.

We are grateful to Myrna Braziel of the RGK Foundation who typed this manuscript and all its revisions. Her remarkable efficiency is surpassed only by her unfailing good will.

The IC^2 Institute at the University of Texas at Austin provided invaluable support. Through research, symposia, conferences, and publications, the Institute has demonstrated its commitment to expanding the base of knowledge about the entrepreneurial process.

We appreciate the interest, encouragement, and help of our editor, Caroline McCarley, at Lexington Books.

Finally, we are grateful to three individuals with great venturing spirits for their patience, understanding, and support—Ronya Kozmetsky, Engracia Gill, and Judy Smilor.

Introduction

Venture capital is practiced in many forms. Indeed, the general understanding of the term "venture capital" makes it difficult to place parameters on the industry. Risk capital, as venture capital is sometimes described, is present in one form or another in almost any venture, from real estate to retailing. Risk capital is the money a person takes out of his savings account to buy an interview suit. It is the money a relative puts into someone's first store. It is the cash from an insurance policy that helps set up an office. It is the money one friend loans or provides to another to do anything. But this is not professional venture capital. Professional venture capital is quite different.

The professional venture capital industry is unique because of the institutionalization of its process within certain well-defined segments of the investment community. This book focuses on the important aspects of professional, institutionalized, venture capital as an industry.

Chapter 1 examines the venture capital process. It defines the role of the venture capitalist and describes investment analysis in the venture capital industry. Technology, talent, and capital are the critical components in investment decisions. Various stages of early and expansion financing for emerging companies pose different limitations, problems, and opportunities for venture capitalists. How these components and stages are assessed and integrated not only determines whether a venture capitalist commits to an enterprise, but also spells success or failure for the venture as it competes in the marketplace.

The venture capital industry is complex and dynamic. No two investment opportunities are identical. As shown in chapter 2, the different motivations for venture capital firms account for the variety of organizational structures found in the industry. These structures take the forms of partnerships, business development companies, subsidiaries, small business investment companies, research and development partnerships, and specialty funds. Each presents advantages and constraints that make it different from the others. Each presents an investment mechanism with its own purposes, techniques, and rewards.

Chapter 3 examines the industry's vital statistics, particularly the demographic characteristics of the industry's individual participants—investors, venture capitalists, entrepreneurs, and government. Venture capitalists seek to protect their investments by providing managerial expertise. They have a definite high technology bent. They generally make disbursements on a wide geographical basis. In this process, the regulatory and tax policies of the federal government have a direct impact on the industry, particularly regarding capital gains.

To take advantage of some of the benefits of the venture capital process, new initiatives have emerged to encourage venture capital firm investment. As explained in chapter 4, several states have established some form of venture capital funding with the primary objective of creating jobs. In addition, innovative new business incubators are being formed to nurture entrepreneurial talent. These incubators provide a variety of critical services to entrepreneurs through community efforts, universities, and the private sector.

The United States has provided a social and cultural framework that has made the venture capital industry a strongly American phenomenon. But venture capital is now receiving increasing attention in countries other than the United States. Against the backdrop of the American experience, chapter 5 assesses the development of venture capital in Japan, Great Britain, Sweden, France, West Germany, and Israel. Constraints and stimulants in each of these countries are affecting the pace and direction of an indigenous venture capital industry.

Venture capital is a critical component of an emerging American phenomenon that we have called technology venturing. Technology venturing, as described in chapter 6, is a collaborative entrepreneurial process for commercializing science and technology through innovative institutional arrangements. In an environment in which the public sector serves as a stimulus for technological development through new federal, state, and local policies, technology venturing can provide many opportunities for the private sector to implement creative financial and managerial mechanisms in order to build new businesses.

The appendixes provide additional perspectives on the venture capital industry. Appendix A analyzes the impact of the industry on a regional economy through a case study of the growth of venture capital in Texas. Appendix B outlines for the entrepreneur the key elements of a business plan with an emphasis on what the venture capitalist looks for in assessing an investment opportunity.

Venture capital is a critical component in commercializing new products and services, especially those which are technology related. This high-risk, high-reward industry provides innovative financing and management to emerging enterprises with the potential for fast growth. Through its contribution to economic diversification, job creation, and entrepreneurial support, it plays an important role in business and economic development.

1
The Venture Capital Process

The venture capital industry is a branch of the investment community which specializes in high-risk equity investments. Most venture capitalists center their attention, and their funds, on emerging companies whose starting or continued expansion is restricted by financial capability. Lacking assets or a proven cash flow, these companies are unable to raise capital from conventional sources, such as commercial banks or the public market, and are therefore attracted to venture capital as an alternative financing method. Companies financed through venture capital are generally in growth industries and often possess state-of-the-art technology as a competitive advantage for expanding market share. As a result, venture-backed companies are not infrequently among the most dynamic companies in an industry. Additionally, these firms are high-growth companies that provide jobs, exports, and taxes.

The Role of Venture Capital

Like the banking industry, the venture capital industry serves as a conduit between investors and investee companies. However, the venture capitalist's participation in the nation's economic process is far more extensive and individual than that of a traditional commercial banker. Whereas the role of a banker can be adequately encapsulated in the term "financial intermediary," the role of the venture capitalist is better described as a "resource manager for business development." As illustrated in figure 1-1, the venture capitalist plays a role in the transformational process of business development by employing the resources of entrepreneurial talent, market demand, and technological prowess.

The mechanism of venture capital management is unique to the investment community. A typical independent private partnership offering might state its investment objectives as follows:

> The objective of the partnership is to generate superior rates of return on invested capital by acquiring equity and debt interests in emerging companies (1) with new technologies, new products, or new services, (2) where new applications of technology or services will enhance an existing business, (3) with new management or new marketing strategies, or (4) which may benefit significantly from an infusion of new financing and financial restructuring.

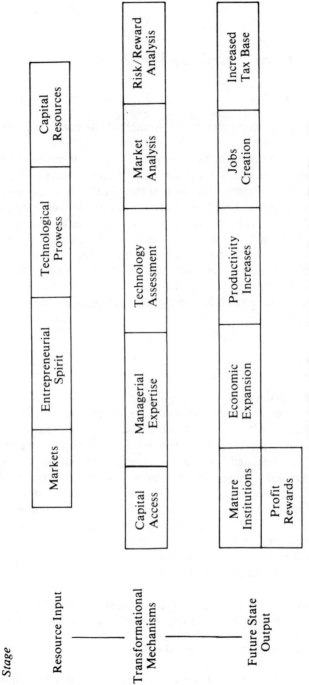

Figure 1–1. Venture Capitalist: Resource Manager for Business Development

The operative description in this statement is the intent to acquire interests in *emerging* companies. Classic capital venturing is widely perceived as the investment in a variety of small, start-up companies whose growth potential is as extraordinary as their risk. This perception does fit the venture capitalist's objective of investing in emerging companies, but it adheres to the preconceived definition of an emerging company as a new or start-up company. This limited preconception is erroneous. An emerging company is most often defined by the venture capitalist as a company already poised to experience robust growth. The venture capitalist does not put parameters on the age or size of a company. Obviously, however, size does limit the ability for future growth because a large firm will experience greater difficulty matching the growth multiples of a small firm. When the opportunity arises to invest in a relatively larger firm, however, venture capitalists do not preclude such involvement out of hand. In either a small or large company, the critical and common element in the selection of investments is the unrecognized potential in some crucial aspect of a company's business.

Most venture capital organizations will put upper and lower limits on their investments, with typical boundaries set at a minimum investment of $500,000 and a maximum investment of 10 percent of committed capital. Often, partnerships will also specify in their offering circulars their investment specialization areas and their participation limits in the management of portfolio companies. Funds specializing in high technology, for example, may state their intent to focus on companies with expertise or products in the following areas:

1. communication technologies,
2. electronics,
3. digital products,
4. financial services,
5. energy conservation devices, or
6. medical and health services and systems.

In a venture capital partnership, the general partner retains the exclusive right either to initiate venture capital investments or to participate in investments led by other venture capital firms. If the partnership initiates the venture capital investment and obtains participation in the financing, then it will probably hold the right to place one or more directors on the target company's board. A lead investor usually has a larger financial commitment than a participating investor. Otherwise, if it participates financially but does not lead the investment, the partnership must be content to let another venture capitalist help manage the company through the board of directors. Private independent partnerships will usually state their investment and management philosophies in the partnership offering. The choice of whether to lead an investment or to participate in an investment initiated by another partnership is a dilemma because it implies a trade-off between management control and diversification of investment. This trade-off results from the fact that a lead investment requires a significantly larger commitment of both available capital and time than does a participation investment. Only the largest firms can overcome this dilemma because sheer size enables simultaneous diversification and management participation.

Venture Capital Analysis

The venture capital process contains three generic components which give the process its own unique role in the analysis of business development investments. As identified in a study by the General Accounting Office, these three components are:

1. technology that meets an identifiable market need;
2. talent that includes not only the entrepreneur, but also business and marketing managers, technologists, scientists, and others; and
3. capital to develop a product or service, fund initial production facilities, and provide early operating capital.[1]

The venture capitalist, of course, arranges for the necessary capital resources to be made available to the investee company. Before an investment is made in a company, however, it must first meet stringent criteria which ensure that the technology and talent components exist. The criteria that venture capitalists employ to analyze an investment's soundness can be categorized under four headings: technical, market, talent, and business planning. Although not all venture capitalists employ the same criteria, these four areas can be considered virtually standard for the industry.

Technical criteria used by venture capitalists aim to assess whether or not the company possesses a unique technology or application of technology that would position it in a potentially fast-growing market. To do so, a new product or process should improve performance, increase the level of service, reduce costs, eliminate equipment needs, and possess the potential to be upgraded as the technology improves. The product or process must be unique and must yield a high profit margin. These last two qualities enable the company to exploit a market niche and to obtain sufficient cash flow for research and development and for expanded operations.

In view of a product life cycle of three to five years, which may be optimistic in some high technology areas, a venture capitalist places much stock in technology that has the potential for further applications. Ideally, products to be developed in the future, using cash flow from present applications of a technology, will use similar distribution channels for marketing. Products and processes that meet all of these technical criteria are often productivity enhancing. This inherent emphasis on productivity is one reason many economists focus on the venture capital process as an important tool in economic development.

Market criteria are distinct from technical criteria in that they address the question of whether or not the product will sell even if the economic need is established under the technical criteria. Venture capitalists look for a near-term identifiable market niche of $50 to $100 million. Though they recognize that a product will not capture 100 percent of this market niche, the market must be large enough to permit both entry and high growth through market share expansion.

Often the venture capitalist will require that the prospective company conduct a survey to ensure the market will accept a new and unique product. Rarely will a venture capitalist accept a company whose product does not have a recognized market. Such an investment has tremendous downside risk; when it is accepted, the product's economic potential must be considerable.

The *talent* criteria, perhaps the most important quality a venture capitalist looks for in a portfolio company, is also one of the most difficult areas to assess. No matter how advanced the technology, it takes considerable skill, dedication, and perseverance by an entrepreneur to market successfully a new product or service under the adverse circumstances of market entry. Management must possess a unique blend of marketing, manufacturing, and finance abilities, and must combine them with an intimate understanding of not only the technology that their company uses, but also the technology commercialization process.

For potential managers who pass the experience and technical knowledge criteria, there is still the question of whether or not they possess the incentive to excel in this position, thereby making both themselves and the venture capitalist significant capital gains. Managers in portfolio companies are expected by venture capitalists to be risk takers with an aversion to losing and a strong desire for personal wealth. Personal integrity and the ability to work with the venture capitalist as a business partner are other essential traits in management. Venture capitalists believe one of the best ways to instill commitment in managers is to require that they make an investment in the company that is significant in size relative to their personal wealth. Such a tactic gives an entrepreneur both personal and professional incentives to excel on the company's behalf.

Many a business proposal will lack the managerial talent required for success, but will otherwise be a sound potential investment. This is often the case in high technology companies where a scientist-inventor will have a viable product but lack the business acumen to make a company work. In this instance, venture capitalists will, through a network of associations and connections, help put together a management team that meets the criteria previously discussed. The process of assembling a management team is a difficult one. Managers who fit the mold are generally in the upper income brackets, hold salaried, career-oriented positions, and enjoy good job security. They are often in the ages between thirty-five to fifty, a period when financial burdens (mortgages and children's education) are traditionally most severe and the risk of abandoning a secure job is at its greatest. The job they are being offered by a venture capitalist represents lower salary and less job security. The primary benefit of a job with a venture capital sponsored firm, however, is the potential reward from stock ownership. This type of incentive, which in the case of a successful company can be substantial indeed, is common; it represents implicit evidence that venture capitalists recognize that success depends significantly on the initiative and drive of all team members.

Venture capitalists do not, however, merely invest money in a portfolio company and then wait for their investment to mature. Rather, they take an active role in the firm. In a venture capital-backed firm, a venture capitalist will almost always hold one directorship and often more. The directorship is held not only because the venture capitalist is a major investor in the company, which would automatically carry board membership anyway, but also because the venture capitalist is unusually experienced and knowledgeable in the maturation process of growing companies. Leaving the day-to-day task of managing the firm to others, venture capitalists use their own expertise to help in such areas as strategic planning, financial advice, policy coordination, and market targeting. A venture capitalist's managerial commitment and financial participation will generally be of the same duration, five to eight years. As a rule of thumb, time constraints limit individual venture capitalists' directorship participation to approximately five or six portfolio companies at a time.

A company's *business plan,* because it represents the prospective implementation of the process where technology and managerial talent are combined to produce a product, is analyzed by the venture capitalist with as much care as either the technology, market, or management criteria. Venture capitalists are not interested in braggadocio. Hence, a venture capitalist expects a business plan that includes realistic cost estimates, market penetration surveys, projected capital requirements, and management resumés, as well as a detailed schematic of the anticipated timing of landmark events. For the venture capitalist, the purpose of the business plan is to ascertain that requisite criteria are acknowledged, accounted for and forecasted using reasonable assumptions. (Appendix B presents the key elements of an effective business plan.)

Venture capitalists look to the business plan to help in the investment valuation. Private independent partnerships aim for a minimum return of 25 to 35 percent per year, with the exceptional partnership garnering up to a 50 percent rate of return per annum. Venture capitalists often will apply the rule of thumb that an investment should have the potential to increase to 500 percent of its original value in three years, a 67 percent rate of return. Although this rule is very strict, the venture capitalist realizes many an investment never reaches its potential. In order to cover the dilution of profits by substandard investments, the venture capital firm must set high standards for all of its investments. Over an eight-year investment cycle, the pool of capital in the private independent partnership, if it is to earn the 30 percent rate of return considered minimum in the industry, must increase eightfold. An average pool of $40 million would, in eight years, increase to $325 million, using a 30 percent multiple.

In an average financing round a portfolio company receives about $2 million. This investment, if it is to increase by a compounded 30 percent, must be worth $12.5 million in seven years. A venture capitalist usually will take no more than 60 percent of a company's equity, leaving the remainder in the hands of the founders and managers as rewards and incentives. Thus, after seven years, the company will have to be worth just under $20 million if the venture capitalist is to receive an adequate reward. Working backwards from this figure, if the company has a price-to-earnings multiple of 13, this means that the company earns approximately $1.5 million. If earnings are 7 percent of sales, then the company has revenues of about $21 million. The venture capitalist will look for figures and assumptions in the business plan which indicate that at a minimum a company can achieve earnings and sales growth which will lead to an organization of this size. Because there will be firms in a venture capitalist's portfolio that fail, these figures are low for a successful venture-backed company. For the profits of a successful venture-backed company to offset a portfolio's losses, the actual figures for the successful company will likely be double those presented here.

Venture capital partnerships will also make nonconventional venture investments. Such investments are still within a partnership's investment objectives. These fall into the category of companies that may benefit significantly from an infusion of new financing or financial restructuring. The two most common of these investments are leveraged buyouts and acquisitions of public companies. Venture capital partnerships generally place the emphasis of their attention on classic capital venture investments, but will nevertheless consider other investment opportunities that will generate superior rates of return. Because leveraged buyouts and acquisitions are not part of conventional capital venturing, the details of the investment methodology used by venture capitalists to evaluate such investment opportunities are presented in chapter 2 under the discussion of specialty funds.

General partners plan on liquidating the partnership's portfolio companies five to seven years following the initial commitment. The two avenues they have to do this are through an upward merger with a larger company or through an initial public stock offering. It is important to realize that the timing of this liquidation is of the utmost importance to the venture capital partnership because the present value of a dollar earned in the future declines rapidly each year. Consider the fact that using a 30 percent discount rate, a dollar earned seven years hence is worth 15.9 cents; in eight years, 12.3 cents; in nine years, 9.4 cents; and in ten years, 7.3 cents. If an investment matures after eight years instead of the projected seven years and has no change in the value at maturation, then in just one year the investment is worth fully 20 percent less than its projected value. From this analysis, it is readily apparent why the projected growth patterns must be maintained. Otherwise, venture capitalist earnings are quickly diluted to the point that investments with lower risk become viable alternatives. Another, external, variable which severely impacts a venture capitalist's investment analysis is inflation. The uncertainty of inflation causes venture capitalists to shorten their investment horizon and avoid longer term commitments.

Even in the absence of such aggravating factors as inflation, venture capitalists are highly selective among the business proposals received. Reportedly, of 200 to 300 business proposals received annually by a venture capital partnership, only 25 to 30 proposals make it past the initial screening process. These 25 to 30 proposals are then given thorough analysis, and 5 of them are funded. Of those companies funded, only 20 percent will achieve the success warranting a public stock offering. Forty percent will achieve success through an upward merger into a large corporation; 20 percent will remain small, privately held businesses; and the final 20 percent will be business failures.[2]

There are various reasons why such a small percentage of business proposals are funded. According to a report by the General Accounting Office:

> The reason so few proposals are financed is a combination of the strict criteria applied, a dearth of or inaccessibility to highly competent management talent, the limited number of portfolio managers, and the risk-reward environment created by government.[3]

Stages of Financing

Venture capitalists rarely invest in public companies. Such companies are generally not part of venture capitalists' investment orientation. Hence, the financing stages of a venture-backed company can be categorized by their pre-initial public offering status. The stages can be defined as follows:

1. *Seed financing*—capital provided to an entrepreneur to prove a concept. It rarely exceeds $50,000. It may include product development but does not involve initial marketing.

2. *Start-up financing*—financing used in product development and initial marketing. Companies may be in the organization process, or they may have been in business a short time (one year or less) but not have sold their product commercially. Usually, such firms would have assembled key management, prepared a business plan, made market studies, and generally prepared themselves to do business.

3. *First-stage financing*—financing provided to companies that have expended their initial capital (often in developing a prototype) and require funds to initiate commercial manufacturing and sales.

4. *Second-stage financing*—working capital used for the initial expansion of a company that is producing and shipping a product and has growing accounts receivable and inventories. Although the company has clearly made progress, it may not be showing a profit as yet.

5. *Third-stage financing*—funds provided for financing major expansion of a company whose sales volume is increasing and that is breaking even or showing a profit. These funds are utilized for further plant expansion, marketing, working capital, or product improvement.

6. *Fourth-stage, mezzanine, or bridge financing*—capital funds invested in a company expecting to go public within six months to a year.[4]

The first three stages should be considered early-stage financing; the last three, expansion financing.

Venture capitalists have an established incentive to invest in each of these financing stages. In theory, a venture capitalist's investments will be heavily weighted toward start-up financing. Though highly risky, start-up investments provide cheaply priced equity issues with potential for exponential growth. Realistically, however, venture capitalists acknowledge the fact that their investment responsibility cannot end with an initial capital infusion. This is because it is in the nature of a business to require increased amounts of working capital as it matures. Such funds are required for financing accounts receivable, inventories, plant expansion, marketing expenses, and so on. To protect their investment or to compensate for the lack of available working capital from traditional sources, venture capitalists provide later stage financing to their successful companies who otherwise would be unable to expand to a profitable maturity stage. Venture capital firms have the additional incentive to support these companies because, as a separate investment opportunity, follow-on financings can be highly profitable. Consider the fact that although a first stage financing in a successful company can yield returns in excess of 100 percent a year, follow-on investments can still yield returns of 40 percent or more, and with a more reasonable amount of risk than that associated with a first-stage financing.

Despite the potential profitability of an investment, the risk borne by a venture capitalist is still significant. Another method venture capitalists use to protect their investment is to assume responsibility for consulting services to their investee company. Pragmatically, they recognize that if they do not use their own resources and expertise to help in the management of a company during a crisis, then they must accept the consequences of other people's efforts. This approach could easily risk an entire investment. Moreover, there are a sufficient number of crises in the normal course of a venture-backed concern to require a venture capitalist to accept as routine the role of consultant.

Venture capitalists, because of their equity position, have an ongoing interest in the health and stability of a fledgling company. The equity interest of a venture capitalist often cannot be liquidated entirely until six months to a year after a company's initial public offering, and possibly longer. Hence, the venture capitalist's goal coincides with societal interests in economic development. That goal is to nurture a promising new company until it achieves a sufficiently mature stage to function as a successful entity in the public marketplace.

The mutuality of interest between venture capital firms and society's concern for economic development is evidenced in a variety of ways. First, venture capital firms enable new ventures to receive funding for innovative projects and ideas. Such firms, whose only assets most often are an idea and a proven managerial expertise, would be unable to obtain funding from the public marketplace, where quantitative analysis holds sway over qualitative analysis, and where short-term orientations overshadow the long-term analysis necessary to the proper germination of an idea. Even if a company were established as a small emerging growth firm, the continuing spotlight of short-term analysis endemic to the public market could stunt the organization's long-term planning ability.

Venture capitalists, whose monetary interests are oriented toward capital gains rather than current income, have a vested incentive to maximize income over a five-to-seven-year period. Their reward comes after a company goes public. Venture capitalists, therefore, work toward positioning a company for the initial public offering and not for interim cash flow. The advantages of this tactic are that the company does not have to satisfy stockholders with dividends; can incur negative cash flows without automatically receiving pressure to change tactics; can reinvest any retained income; and can, in effect, allow its management to concentrate on product development. Society also benefits from this tactic because this longer-term orientation enables companies to become stable, productive, organizations before they reach the marketplace.

Notes

1. U.S. General Accounting Office, *Government-Industry Cooperation Can Enhance the Venture Capital Process,* GAO/AMFD-82-35, August 12, 1982, p. 15.

2. Ibid., p. 2.

3. Ibid., p. 15.

4. "Venture Capitalists Invest \$2.8 Billion in 1983," *Venture Capital Journal,* May 1984, p. 9.

2
Motivations and Structures: The Nature of the Venture Capital Industry

T o understand the venture capital industry it is necessary to realize that no two investments made by a venture capital firm are identical. Because the industry recognizes no single set of rules and procedures for investment as valid, it is impossible to present a universal and all-inclusive definition and categorization of the industry. Chapter 1 presented a description of the industry's dominant investment process, a description valid for a large majority of venture capital transactions. Nevertheless, exceptions to conventional venture capital investment procedures are common. Even within the mainstream of conventional venture capital investment, variations are the rule rather than the exception.

One reason for the complex nature of the venture capital industry is the different motivations possessed by the various venture capital organizations within the industry. The motivations of a venture capitalist firm are influenced by a variety of factors, including its:

1. tax category,
2. regulatory constraints, and
3. organizational constraints.

Knowledge of various organizational structures can aid in understanding a venture capitalist's rationale for investing in a company. Such knowledge provides insight into the structures venture capitalists employ for their investments, and why variations from what is considered conventional venture investing occur. This chapter examines the organizational structures and constraints faced by selected segments of the venture capital industry. The industry segments to be examined are:

1. private independent venture capital partnerships (referred to as partnerships);
2. corporate venture capital subsidiaries (subsidiaries);
3. public venture capital companies (business development companies, or BDCs);
4. small business investment companies (SBICs);

5. research and development partnerships (R&D partnerships); and
6. specialty funds.

In 1983, partnerships controlled $8.5 billion of venture capital funds; subsidiaries controlled $2.4 billion; BDCs controlled $500 million; and SBICs controlled $890 million of private capital and $826 million of leverage from the Small Business Administration. Because partnerships controlled over 66 percent of funds available for venture capital investment at year end 1983, partnerships will be the first industry segment to be examined. It will then be possible to describe the practices of other segments of the venture capital industry in relation to the venture capital partnership.

Private Independent Venture Capital Partnerships

Tax benefits and legal constraints provide the major reasons for setting up a limited partnership. The partnership has a general partner, usually the venture capitalist's investment firm, which manages the partnership's investment portfolio. The fund's limited partners, its investors, most often are passive. Since a typical venture capital investment has a time horizon of five to seven years, most partnership funds set eight to ten years as their lifetime, with the general partner holding the option to extend this lifetime by up to 3 one-year periods. The option for additional time periods ensures the orderly dissolution of the fund's investments, generally for those companies that have not sufficiently matured for public distribution.

A typical partnership formed in 1983 would have been funded with $40 million. Limited partners would be required to invest a minimum of $1 million, with the general partner reserving the right to accept smaller participations. The fund would become operable when commitments of $15 million were received; if an upper limit of $60 million were achieved, no further commitments would be accepted. The general partner of the partnership would be paid an annual management fee of 2.5 percent of committed capital, and would in addition receive an incentive allocation of 20 percent of the fund's realized net gains. The limited partners would be allocated the remaining 80 percent of net gains.

Ordinary income of the typical partnership, such as income from dividends or interest, is allocated 80 percent to the limited partners in accordance with their respective capital accounts, and 20 percent to the general partner. These funds are paid only after fees and expenses incurred by the general partner are covered, and are distributed annually. Income from capital transactions, allocated to the limited and general partners in a similar manner, is distributed upon termination of the partnership. For tax purposes, all gains are allocated to the limited partners when they occur, and even though these partners receive no income, they have a tax obligation for this income. A limited partner, therefore, must have adequate income not only to participate in the funding of the partnership, but also to meet independently the tax liability incurred by participation in the partnership. An investment in a venture capital firm is illiquid and often nontransferable.

The organization of the venture capital partnership enables venture capital funds to move between investors and investments and is structured to take maximum advantage of the incentives to invest in venture capital. Venture capital is most often organized into partnerships in order to avoid corporate income taxes. Any ordinary income is first used to cover expenses incurred so that ordinary income taxes are minimized. The emphasis by venture capitalists on capital gains over ordinary income is designed to take advantage of the lower capital gains tax and the compounding of interest without taxes permitted under federal law.

In the case of the private independent partnerships, venture capitalists are highly remunerated for their services. Indeed, a 2.5 percent management fee and 20 percent of profits can become a considerable amount of money over ten years. This incentive also ensures that the highest caliber of personnel is attracted to the position of general partner.

Corporate Venture Capital Subsidiaries

Venture capital firms that are nonpublic subsidiaries of large corporations represent a major facet of the venture capital industry. Although in 1983 this segment of the industry controlled only 32 percent as much capital as private partnerships controlled, many of the firms are among the largest venture capital institutions in the country.[1] Four of the top ten most active venture capital investors in 1983 were corporate subsidiaries whose parent companies were Allstate Insurance Company, First National Bank of Chicago, General Electric Corporation, and Citicorp. In 1983 these four companies, through their subsidiaries, invested $305.2 million.[2]

Corporate subsidiaries are organized in a variety of ways. The firm may be organized as a partnership in a manner similar to a private independent partnership, with the corporation being the sole limited partner. The firm may also be set up as a separate wholly owned corporation. Finally, the subsidiary may actually be a division of the parent company, similar to the trust department in a bank or the investment department in an insurance company. In any case, the parent company is the sole investing participant in the corporate venture capital subsidiary (hereafter referred to simply as subsidiary).

Like private partnerships, subsidiaries will invest in a wide variety of areas and will consider almost any viable investment that has the potential to yield a superior rate of return. There are exceptions to this generalization, however, as evidenced by Banker's Trust of New York, which specializes in leveraged buyouts. Another similarity to the partnership is the profit objective of the subsidiary. To take advantage of the lower capital gains tax rate, the subsidiary tries to minimize dividend income and maximize long-term capital gains. A subsidiary is generally an ongoing concern and does not liquidate its investments after a specified time period. It nevertheless pays profits on a schedule determined by the corporate parent. Although the organization does have the ability to borrow funds, future growth of a subsidiary generally comes either through income or internal funds.

Business Development Companies

Business development companies (BDCs) are a hybrid of private venture capital funds and publicly owned closed-end investment companies. As venture investors, business development companies have the same investment orientation as private independent partnerships. Because they are organized as public corporations, as compared to private partnerships, however, public venture capital firms fall into a separate category. In addition, because these corporations were created by special legislation through which they gain their legal designation as business development companies, they are regulated by the Securities and Exchange Commission (SEC). These separate tax and regulatory laws cause business development companies to have investment and profit orientations that are somewhat unique when compared to private independent venture capital partnerships.

As previously noted, taxes on realized gains in a partnership are assessed to the limited partners whether or not such gains are distributed. A BDC, by comparison, is taxed only on realized income not distributed in kind. This tax status creates a variety of unique incentives for business development corporations. Like partnerships, BDCs try to limit dividend income because it is taxed to shareholders at the higher ordinary-income tax rate. These organizations also try to limit their corporate net income to zero. When a BDC does distribute dividends, it attempts to do so with nontaxable dividends in kind, which most often take the form of stock. Moreover, ownership in a BDC has the advantage over a partnership in that income is not taxed until distributed, and then it is taxed as income to the shareholders. In most ordinary corporations, dividends are paid out of after-tax income.

As in other public corporations, managers in a BDC must be concerned with the company's stock price. This price is largely a function of the company's net asset value, a statistic computed in a manner similar to a closed-end mutual fund. Net asset value is essentially assets at market value less liabilities, divided by shares outstanding. BDC stock will vary considerably in price relative to net asset value and may sell either at a discount or at a premium. Table 2–1, which lists the public venture capital companies, illustrates this point. For those companies whose shares sell at a discount, capital availability through an equity offering is not a viable option, as stock sales at market value would dilute the net asset value of current shareholders.

Unlike closed-end mutual funds, however, BDCs can borrow money: up to 50 percent of assets and in some cases more. This ability to leverage their funds enhances a BDC's capability to support its portfolio companies and finance new ventures. As public concerns, business development companies can also finance investments and acquisitions through stock swaps. BDCs, however, must also be somewhat conservative and prudent in their investments, as management must answer to both its stockholders and the SEC. This liability affects a BDC's investment philosophy. Although aggressive in comparison to closed-end mutual funds, a BDC's investment philosophy is likely to be more conservative than either a partnership or a subsidiary. BDCs invest only in areas where high growth is assured and shy away from less certain growth products. An example of a BDC's portfolio would likely include investments in information technologies, medical products, consumer products and services, industrial automation, and other high technology, high-growth areas. Although these are areas where partnerships also invest, BDCs limit themselves to these areas while partnerships will consider other investments. Consequently, a BDC's portfolio choice is not as random as is that of the venture capital partnership.

Like a partnership, a BDC actively participates in a portfolio company's management. Unlike a partnership, a BDC nevertheless must, by law, make available this managerial assistance and does not have the option merely to take a small equity interest without contributing actively to the company's management. The Small Business Investment Incentive Act of 1980 requires that a business development company acquire a minimum of 25 percent equity interest in each portfolio company and that it actively participate in the company's management.

A BDC does not liquidate itself after a prespecified amount of time; it is an ongoing concern. To grow, a BDC must do so either through income, borrowing, or a public equity offering. It cannot liquidate one partnership and then start a new venture pool as can a partnership. Since common stock offerings would dilute the stockholder's equity in BDCs, whose stock sells at a discount, these organizations raise equity through off-balance-sheet methods. Additionally, since income not distributed is taxed, thereby reducing potential profits to shareholders, this method of growth is not a preferred approach. While cash income can be protected from taxes by loss carryforwards, this practice cannot effectively increase a company's size. Hence, BDCs manage the affairs of their portfolio companies in such a way that they increase in value without producing significant taxable earnings. Additionally, BDCs

Table 2–1
Statistics of Publicly Held SBICs and Venture Companies

	Total Assets[a]		1966–83 Price Range		06/29/84 Market Bid Price	Price Change From Last Month	Last Reported Net Asset Value Per Share	Market Price to Value Per Share	Earnings[b] Per Share Last Fiscal Year	Div. Per Share
	Market Value	Cost	High	Low						
SBICs										
Capital Corp. of America	$ 2.3	$ 2.2	8¾	⅛	½[h]	+ ⅛	$ 2.24	22%	$ (.03)	$ —
Capital Investments, Inc.	12.8	12.5	14½	1½	3½	—	6.07	58	.03	—
Clarion Capital Corp.	26.2	21.8	18½	2	4½	—	9.40	48	1.09	—
DASBIC, Inc.	27.3	15.0	35	4¼	34¼	− ¾	32.54	105	9.62	—
First Connecticut SBIC	33.4	38.8	24	7⅛	9⅞[h]	− ¼	9.25	107	1.95	.25[e]
The Franklin Corporation	29.0	26.3	16¼	2⅛	12½[h]	− 2	18.79	67	1.51	1.35[f]
Greater Wash. Investors, Inc.	28.4	18.6	23½	⅛	5¾	+ ¼	8.09	71	2.85	.25
Monmouth Capital Corp.	10.2	7.9	12½	2	6¼[h]	—	10.52	59	1.56	.40[f]
Vega Capital Corp.	8.6	9.0	2½	⅜	⅞	—	3.68	24	.01	—
Average SBIC						− 1.4%		62%		
Venture Capital Companies										
Allied Capital Corp.[d]	54.4	40.7	25½	3½	18½	—	13.09	141	2.34	1.40
Biotech Capital Corp.[d]	17.5	14.5	11¼	2⅛	2⅛[h]	− ⅛	4.15	51	1.10	—
Capital Southwest Corp.[d]	53.3	26.2	16¼	⅞	15¼	− ½	19.78	77	1.12	.16[g]
First Midwest Corporation[d]	11.1	10.5	8	¼	5¼[h]	− ¼	7.42	71	(.04)	—
Heizer Corporation	239.1	100.5	17½	7⅞	17¼	+ ¾	20.27	85	(6.25)[c]	—
Midland Capital Corp.[d]	29.1	23.4	16½	1⅛	14¼	− 1	12.40	115	1.34	—
Narragansett Capital Corp.[d]	79.5	61.1	47¼	1⅜	45¼	+ 1½	30.72	147	8.05	.80[e]
The Nautilus Fund	16.5	12.7	51½	11⅜	31½	+ 1	22.57	140	1.76	.39[f]
Rand Capital Corp.[d]	10.0	9.4	16	1	8½[h]	− ½	13.76	62	1.23	.875
Average Venture Company						− 1.8%		99%		

Source: *Venture Capital Journal,* July, 1984, p. 22.

[a]Total assets are computed at both cost and at market value which reflects changes in market value of investments.

[b]Earnings reported are after taxes and reserves for losses including changes in unrealized appreciation (depreciation) of investments.

[c]Includes realized and unrealized gain in investments before extraordinary item (elimination of deferred tax reserve).

[d]Has wholly owned SBIC subsidiary

[e]Quarterly dividend

[f]Annual dividend

[g]Capital gain distribution

[h]Last available quote.

prefer to take their profits in the form of capital gains rather than as dividend income, thereby minimizing their tax burden. The capital-gains tax liability is not incurred until the security is sold either by the company or by its stockholders; in either case, the basis used for tax computation is the BDC's original cost.

BDCs are finding it increasingly difficult to compete as regulated entities in the venture capital industry. In January of 1984, the managers of Narragansett Capital Corporation announced a buyout offer by which they would take the company private. Reportedly the impetus behind the move is the burdensome regulations imposed by the SEC.[3] One rule cited as an example of the bureaucracy BDCs face is the rule by which BDCs must receive SEC permission to invest with "affiliated" persons. Since a company is classified as affiliated when the BDC owns in excess of 5 percent of its stock, many portfolio companies fall into this classification. In order to make a follow-on investment in a portfolio company, therefore, the BDC must obtain SEC permission.

Heizer Corporation, the nation's largest BDC, decided to liquidate in the face of proposed tax status changes. Two separate tax treatments of distributions by BDCs have been proposed. One proposal would make distribution of dividends-in-kind taxable at the corporate level at a capital-gains rate to the extent of its appreciation. The second proposal essentially would view all distributions by the BDC as dividends, and tax them accordingly. In either case, were the regulations adopted they would reduce the after-tax value of shareholders' equity by 25 to 50 percent. Heizer decided to liquidate before the proposed taxes could affect the distribution of its assets as nontaxed dividends-in-kind, thereby realizing for its shareholders the full asset value of the corporation.

Small Business Investment Companies (SBICs)

Government-backed but privately owned, Small Business Investment Companies (SBICs) represent a form of venture capital designed to help small businesses arrange alternative financing. SBICs were created by an act of Congress in 1958, and are licensed and regulated through the Small Business Administration. Limited by law in their investment scope to SBA-defined small businesses, SBICs are for-profit concerns that make long-term financing available to small firms at favorable market rates.

An SBIC derives its initial capitalization from private sources and normally becomes eligible to obtain funds from the government or from private financial institutions through government-guaranteed loans. In this manner, an SBIC may qualify to leverage its capitalization and paid-in surplus by three times, and in certain circumstances, by four times. With this financing ability, an SBIC can either make equity investments in small businesses or make loans to these companies with a minimum five-year maturity schedule. Prepayments are made without penalty and at the borrower's option. The government's interest in supplying this leveraging ability is to make financing available to small businesses unable fully to collateralize conventional borrowings. SBICs make subordinated and unsecured loans to companies with significant profit potential; the same companies could not qualify for long-term financing from either banks or the private equity market.

Investors in SBICs run the gamut from private individuals to corporate subsidiaries to publicly traded stocks. In 1983, commercial banks owned interests in 86 SBICs, 74 of which were controlled by the banks. Nonfinancial corporations owned 45 SBICs, other financial corporations controlled 26 SBICs, and 19 SBICs were publicly traded. In 1983, private individuals held 192 of the 368 SBICs reporting to the SBA.[4]

Because of SBA regulations, an SBIC's investment policies are far more restrictive than those of any other venture capital institution. An SBIC may only invest in a business whose net worth does not exceed $6 million and whose average net income after taxes for each of the preceding two years is less than $2 million. An SBIC may invest a maximum of 20 percent of paid-in capital and surplus in a single small business, and may invest a maximum of 33 percent of its portfolio in real estate investments. Foreign investment is not allowed for an SBIC, nor can an SBIC make funds available to a small business for relending. All firms an SBIC invests in or lends to must conduct regular and continuous business activity. Investments contrary to the public interest are also disallowed.

SBICs may borrow funds, and the SBA will either guarantee or lend the SBIC these funds when capital is unavailable from private sources. SBICs are eligible for SBA loans of three times their capital and paid-in surplus. For SBICs with private capital equal to or in excess of $500,000, funds equivalent to 400 percent of private capital become available if 65 percent of the total funds available for investment are invested in or committed to venture capital investments. The maximum leverage available to an SBIC is $35 million.

As an incentive to investors to form SBICs, Congress has legislated many tax advantages for SBICs that are not enjoyed by other investment institutions. An SBIC shareholder is permitted to treat gains on sales of SBIC stock as long-term capital gains. Furthermore, such a shareholder may take an unlimited ordinary-loss deduction on losses arising from sale, exchange, or worthlessness of the SBIC stock. SBICs are allowed a deduction of 100 percent of dividends received from a taxable domestic corporation, rather than the 85 percent deduction allowed most corporate taxpayers. SBICs are granted relief from the tax on excess accumulations of surplus capital and may qualify for relief from the tax on personal holding companies. Additionally, specific provisions in the Internal Revenue Code exist that allow SBICs to take full deductions against ordinary income for losses sustained on convertible debentures, or on stock received through conversion of convertible debentures.

These tax provisions and investment restrictions give SBICs a profit goal unique to the venture capital industry. Whereas other venture capital firms try to minimize dividend income and surplus cash, SBICs have no need to do so unless the portfolio company's projected internal rate of return is greater than the SBIC's opportunity rate of return. Since SBICs have access to significant amounts of leveraged funds, and since any losses on many debt instruments are fully tax deductible as ordinary income, SBICs have an incentive to make investments with higher risk horizons. Such investments have an upside potential for high returns, and the downside risk is significantly cushioned by ordinary income tax loss regulations.

Because of regulations limiting investment to small businesses, SBICs commonly make smaller disbursements to portfolio companies than do other segments of the venture capital industry. SBICs can grow through SBA leveraging and through additional paid-in capital.

SBICs share a common problem with BDCs: both are regulated entities subject to the vagaries of politics. SBICs and BDCs are attractive alternatives to venture capital partnerships only because of benefits legislated expressly to encourage their development. Legislation not specifically intended to affect SBICs and BDCs nevertheless often does so, and the result is often negative. SBICs and BDCs can therefore be legislated out of existence just as rapidly as they were legislated into existence, and in a far more random manner.

An example of the random nature of adverse legislation is a change in the tax laws included in the 1984 Deficit Reduction Act. Before the Deficit Reduction Act, distributions of stock by SBICs to shareholders were not taxed. Since the act was passed, any distributions of stock by incorporated SBICs is taxed at the corporate level as capital gains and at the shareholder level as ordinary income. Effectively this reduces the value of SBIC stock by nearly a third, since that is the additional tax burden shareholders will pay. Incorporated SBICs will likely be reorganized as partnerships and some will undoubtedly liquidate, having been legislated out of existence. This attrition of venture capital vehicles makes the rise of research and development partnerships, a new form of venture capital, highly significant.

Research and Development Limited Partnerships

The research and development (R&D) limited partnership is the newest and fastest-growing segment of the venture capital industry. Though feasible since a precedent-setting court decision in 1974, R&D partnerships only became common in 1981 after major investment-banking firms utilized this financing method to fund a few large projects.[5] In that year, $160 million of venture financing was arranged through the R&D partnership vehicle.[6] In 1982, this figure is estimated to have ballooned to between $500 and $600 million, and by 1990 it is projected to reach $2.5 billion per year.[7]

The motivating factors behind the rapid development of this industry segment are clear. Investors, the limited partners in an R&D partnership, receive the rights to two significant R&D benefits: (1) the tax deduction for research and development expenses incurred by the partnership, which can total 99 percent of the investment; and (2) royalties, licensing fees, or capital gains from any technology developed in the course of the partnership's research.

The sponsoring company, which usually acts directly or through a proxy as the partnership's general partner, benefits significantly from the R&D partnership in the following manner: (1) the company shifts the high costs and risks of research and development to the partnership, yet retains ultimate control over the developed technology; and (2) the company can pursue research and development without sacrificing equity or incurring debt.

It is evident, then, that R&D partnerships fill the needs of both investors and companies seeking to fund R&D. Investors use a fifty cent (after tax) dollar and in return receive the rights to potentially lucrative technology. Sponsoring companies control R&D without sacrificing equity or increasing debt, and only pay for developed technology if it is successful.

An R&D partnership is usually a highly complicated structure due to the necessity of accommodating the desires of all the participants. To garner an initial understanding of the R&D partnership as a venture capital vehicle, one must understand the interplay of the four components to an R&D partnership. The four components are:

1. the limited partnership,
2. the sponsoring company,
3. the research and development contract, and
4. the buyout arrangement.

The limited partnership is the structure most often used by R&D partnerships. The beneficial tax treatment afforded the limited partners is the primary reason for the limited partnership, with the limited liability incurred being a second consideration. Partnerships, unlike corporations, are not taxable entities. Items of partnership income and loss are allocated to the limited partners, who then combine them with other items of income or loss on their individual tax returns. Any tax benefits to the partnership, consequently, flow through to the limited partners on a prorata basis.

The sponsoring company is the organization that wants to fund an R&D project. While possessing some expertise in a base technology, the sponsoring company lacks the funds to develop new technology internally. The R&D partnership is the vehicle that enables the sponsoring company both to fund research and development in its field and to control that R&D without sacrificing equity control or assuming a large debt burden. The sponsoring company initiates the R&D partnership; determines the specifics of the partnership agreement; acts as the general partner or creates a subsidiary to act as the general partner; reserves contractually an option on the technology developed by the partnership's research; and contributes the base technology necessary to commence research and development.

The research and development contract, which specifies the company that will carry out the actual R&D work, sets the compensation for the research carried out, which is usually performed on a best efforts basis (no guaranteed results). The contract remunerates the company performing the R&D on either a fixed-fee or a cost-plus basis. The R&D contract is important to the structure of the partnership because it enables tax deductions to be taken in the year the partnership makes payments for R&D. Hence, using a prepaid R&D contract, limited partners receive all their tax deductions in one year. For investors in the 50 percent tax bracket, this reduces the net amount at risk and doubles the effective rate of return. This tax advantage also benefits the sponsoring company, since investors will accept a lower rate of return for their dollar than if they were shareholders in a corporation.

The buyout arrangement, which is predetermined and set forth in the partnership agreement, enables the sponsoring company to acquire the rights to the developed technology. To acquire the rights to this technology, the sponsoring company will usually structure its payments to the limited partners in one of three ways.

First, in the *royalty partnership* method, the sponsoring company holds the option to an exclusive license of the technology for manufacturing and marketing purposes. In exchange the sponsoring company pays the partnership royalties at rates that range between 6 and 10 percent of gross sales. There may be an upper limit on the cumulative royalty payments, or the company may have the option to purchase the technology in return for a prespecified lump-sum payment.

Second, in the *equity partnership* method, the sponsoring company and the limited partners agree to form a new corporation after the technology is developed. The partnership interests are converted into equity in a tax-free transaction at a rate based on a predetermined formula. This type of partnership is designed to launch new companies, and closely resembles a venture capital investment. This structure is unique because it enables venture capital oriented investors to take advantage of favorable tax benefits.

A third buyout method is the *joint venture*, in which the R&D partnership contributes the successfully developed technology, and the sponsoring company contributes the manufacturing and marketing expertise. Both participants then share equally in the venture's profits. At some point either the partnership or, more likely, the sponsoring company, pursuant to cross-purchase options in the joint venture agreement, will purchase the other participant's interests. Though similar in some respects to the royalty buyout, the joint venture buyout minimizes the sponsoring company's early outlays and allows it to perfect marketing and manufacturing operations without being burdened by large royalty payments.

When creatively used, the R&D partnership has many venture capital applications. It fulfills the need of emerging companies to fund research and development without mortgaging their future, and provides investors with tax-sheltered investment opportunities. As in any venture investment, there are the technical, market, managerial and planning risks discussed in chapter 1 of this study. R&D partnerships have one further risk, however, a financial risk. There is no guarantee that either the money raised to fund a project will be sufficient to complete the development of a technology, or that additional money can be raised to complete a project whose funding falls short of that necessary to complete its goal.

For the sponsoring company there are disadvantages as well as advantages. The advantages include transfer of risk, retention of R&D control, reacquisition rights, a lack of stock dilution, and no unfavorable accounting impacts. An R&D partnership, however, is expensive to establish and royalty payments can be onerous if not set at reasonable levels. Also, over a four- to six-year period, an R&D partnership can be more expensive than debt on a successfully developed project since interest expense on debt is tax-deductible and the tax deduction on R&D expenditures is lost. An R&D partnership is generally less expensive than equity.[8]

Specialty Funds

Many venture capital firms actively invest in opportunities where a company's financial and organizational restructuring is the primary activity that leads an investment to realize capital gains. This tactic, because it sharply differs from the classic venture capital activity of building an emerging company into a viable public market entity, has been called "capital vulturing," an adulterated form of capital venturing. Yet many venture capitalists practice this investment strategy and believe that their services are beneficial to a healthy economy. The types of investment that fall under the heading of "financial and organizational restructuring" are management leveraged buyouts, acquisitions, and mergers; many venture capital firms concentrate in these specialties. Because many venture capital firms will actively pursue financial reconstruction as an investment activity, it is important to detail the criteria employed for investment analysis. This discussion focuses on management-leveraged buyouts, an investment area that in 1982 received over $140 million of venture capital disbursements and in 1983 received over $250 million of venture capital disbursements.[9]

The term "management-leveraged buyout" (LBO) refers to the acquisition of an existing company by a new corporation formed by the acquiror for that sole purpose and funded with substantial amounts of institutional debt relative to the contributed equity. The ratio of debt to equity immediately following an acquisition of this nature may be as high as 10 to 1. Factors influencing the actual debt-to-equity ratio include the nature of the acquired business, the confidence of the acquiror and the lending institutions in the cash generating capacity of the target company, and the target company's capacity to meet its financial obligations in a timely fashion.

Because of the substantial amounts of leverage involved in a management-leveraged buyout, the common stock of the newly established company carries a valuation that is extremely low relative to future earnings potential, historic earnings records, and underlying asset values. A venture capitalist's function in the leveraged buyout is to arrange the financing for the company and to place the equity securities with private investors. The venture capitalist will purchase a substantial portion of this low-priced equity. The greatest financial risk involved in a company acquired through a management-leveraged buyout is the owner's equity investment. In the case of bankruptcy, owner's equity is subordinated to all other claims on the organization. Yet the owner's equity also is the only instrument with upside potential in an LBO. Hence, venture capitalists use equity as an incentive instrument and make sure that all interested parties in the transaction have a share.

By far the most important factor in the success of an LBO is the commitment, quality, perseverance, and consistent performance of the target company's management team. To ensure that the commitment of an acquired company's management is equal to the tasks at hand, a venture capitalist will insist that the management purchase a meaningful equity share. Because the financing of an LBO is so important to its outcome, venture capitalists also like to have the lending institutions participate in the equity financing. Such a tactic gives the lending institution an additional incentive to make the firm a profitable, self-sufficient, ongoing concern. In such cases, the purpose of equity participation by management, lending institutions, and venture capitalists is to create a capital structure in which all parties to the acquisition play a constructive role in the future success of the target company. Such a capital structure creates a common set of financial and operating goals among all parties to the transaction. These goals are to build up the fundamental underlying value of the target company and to maximize the long-term capital appreciation of the equity securities purchased by the investors.

Candidates for LBO transactions generally fall into one of three categories:

1. publicly traded companies, in which case the LBO constitutes a "going private" transaction;
2. privately held companies, in which case the LBO constitutes a simple acquisition; and
3. divisions or subsidiaries of larger corporations, in which case the LBO creates an independent and free-standing enterprise.

Publicly held companies are prime candidates for LBOs when the value the securities market places on the individual company does not reflect that company's intrinsic value. This situation happens when a company, because of the need to satisfy stockholder demands for consistent quarterly earnings-per-share ratios, sacrifices long-term goals for short-term achievements, thereby stunting the company's true long-term earnings potential. An LBO can return the company's market value to its fundamental corporate value through renewed strategic forms and new entrepreneurial management.

An LBO transaction allows management to focus on building a company's ability to grow and provide cash flow. The public market gains a cash price for its shares in a target company and also receives a premium over the market price. Moreover, management gains renewed incentive to build the company because of its equity participation.

Privately held companies are LBO candidates when owners of their closely held stock expect to divest themselves of the company. As private companies, however, they would have difficulties with an initial public offering; only a small portion of the company's stock could be offered initially, and the after market for the stock is highly uncertain. An alternative to the public market would be to sell out to a larger corporation, often a competitor. This alternative is often unsatisfactory, as the owner of the smaller corporation frequently will not receive cash for the company. Consequently, selling out to a competitor is often viewed by an entrepreneur–owner as an admission that the owner's company is second rate.

An LBO is often a viable alternative to these two approaches. The owner of a private company, often the entrepreneur who built the company, can receive a cash price for the business and can sell it to the management who helped build it. The company remains private, and the owner enjoys personal and financial satisfaction.

Divisions and subsidiaries are LBO candidates when senior managers determine that, for strategic reasons, they should sell these portions of the company. In such a case, an LBO enables the parent company to realize full market price, often in cash, for its division or subsidiary without selling to a competitor. At the same time, it creates an atmosphere of goodwill throughout the parent company because the division or subsidiary's executives were given the opportunity to purchase the business under their management. Also, the parent company has the opportunity to sell its subsidiary or division in a discreet manner, with a minimum of management disruption within the subsidiary or division or the parent company.

Table 2–2 summarizes the various goals and orientations of the venture capital industry. In addition, "incubators," an emerging concept in the industry, are listed here but discussed in chapter 4.

In addition to the various organizational structures and investment criteria, there is another important facet of the venture capital industry. The

Table 2–2
Goals and Orientation: Summary of Value Capital Industry Segments

	Private Independent VC Partnership	Public Venture Capital Corp (BD)	Corporate Venture Capital Subsidiary	Small Business Investment Companies	Specialty Funds	R&D Partnerships	Incubators
Investors	Private	Public	Private subsidiary	Corporate/private	Private	Public/private	Public/private
Investment strategies	Random	Random	Random	Small business	Specialty	Pre-determined	Seed stage
Borrowing	Seldom	Often	Internal	Government sponsored	Various	Seldom	Seldom
Profit goals	Capital gains	Dividends in-kind	Capital gains	Capital gains/income	Capital gains	Capital gains/royalty income	Capital gains/royalty income
Dividend policy	None	Variable, payment in-kind	As received	Variable	None, Variable	Pre-determined	Variable
Liquidation	7–10 yrs.	Ongoing	Ongoing	Ongoing	Variable	3–6 yrs. to buyout	Ongoing/variable
Taxes	Taxed as partnership	No tax on div. in-kind (current)	Corporate	Special provisions	Variable	Taxed as a partnership	Variable
Future growth	New fund	Borrowing	Income	Variable	Variable	None	None

next chapter examines the relation of demographics to the mechanisms employed by venture capitalists to raise funds, develop potential investments, and disburse risk capital to entrepreneurs.

Notes

1. "Venture Capitalists Invest $2.8 Billion in 1983," *Venture Capital Journal*, May 1984, p. 9.
2. "The Venture Capital 100," *Venture*, June 1984, p. 61.
3. Johnnie L. Roberts, "Narragansett Managers Offer to Buy Concern," *Wall Street Journal*, January 23, 1984, p. 14.
4. U.S. Small Business Administration, Investment Division, *Directory of Operating Small Business Investment Companies*, December 1983, p. 63.
5. The decision leading to the authorization of the partnership vehicle for financing research and development occurred in the case of *Snow* v. *Commissioner* [Edwin A. Snow, 416 US 500 (1974) (33 AFTR2d 74-1251, 74-1 USTC para. 9432)]. This case contested the IRS interpretation of Section 174 of the Internal Revenue Code. Section 174 allows a taxpayer to expense research and development costs in the year those expenses occur, rather than forcing the taxpayer to capitalize those expenses over a period determined by IRS schedules, usually over a 3 to 5 year period beginning in the year initial revenues from the product are received. The IRS had narrowly interpreted this section as being applicable only to taxpayers carrying on a trade or business and actively offering a product or service for sale. The *Snow* decision changed this interpretation so that in order to qualify for Section 174 treatment, a taxpayer need only incur substantial business risks and have a reasonable expectation of profit. In this instance, the taxpayer is considered to meet the requirement of being in connection with a trade or business. Since tax benefits and liabilities are passed through the partnership directly to the partner, this means an individual can receive the tax benefits associated with the partnership's research and development expenditures, and that the limited partner's investment at risk is immediately reduced by an amount commensurate with his tax bracket, presumably 50 percent. For a clear explanation of the tax consequences of the research and development partnership vehicle, see *Forming R&D Partnerships: An Entrepreneur's Guidebook*, by Anthony P. Spohr and Leslie Wat, and available from the accounting offices of Deloitte, Haskins & Sells.
6. Anise C. Wallace, "Magic Financing Via R&D Partnerships," *High Technology*, July 1983, p. 65.
7. Anthony C. Spohr, and Leslie Wat, *Forming R&D Partnerships: An Entrepreneur's Guidebook* (No city given: Deloitte, Haskins & Sells, 1983), p. 3.
8. Ibid., p. 33.
9. "Venture Capitalists Invest," p. 10.

3
The Demographics of the Venture Capital Industry

T he previous two chapters have examined the characteristics and objectives of venture capital investing and the industry participants whose organizations and aspirations form its unique character. This chapter examines the structure of the industry from demographic and statistical perspectives. It is organized by participants in the venture capital process, as defined in chapter 1. They are:

1. investors,
2. venture capitalists,
3. entrepreneurs, and
4. the federal government.

Investors

Of the $3.4 billion committed to independent private capital venture partnerships in 1983, 31 percent was from pension funds. This total confirmed pension funds as the major contributor to independent partnerships. Of the $8.5 billion controlled by partnerships, pension funds committed nearly $2 billion, and half of that total was committed in 1983.[1] Since the total investment pool of pension funds in 1983 was greater than $900 billion, the $2 billion invested in venture capital pools from 1977 to 1983 represents two-tenths of one percent of investable funds. As illustrated in table 3-1, the other sources in the funding of venture capital pools are individuals and families, insurance companies, foreign investors, corporations, endowments, and foundations.

It is noteworthy that this list does not include the contributions of many corporate, family, and bank venture groups that invest their own capital and do not raise outside funds. Because they do not raise outside funds, these groups are neither required to nor choose to disclose their pool size, commitments, disbursements, or investments. Specific information concerning their activities is not readily available. These investors in the venture capital process often provide large pools of capital and manage this capital in much the same fashion as do private independent venture capital pools. For example,

Table 3-1
Capital Commitments, 1980 and 1983 (Independent Private Partnerships Only)

	Total Capital Committed (millions of dollars)				Percent of Total Capital Committed			
	1980	1981	1982	1983	1980	1981	1982	1983
Pension Funds	197	200	474	1,070	30	23	33	31
Individuals and Families	102	201	290	707	16	23	21	21
Insurance Companies	88	132	200	410	13	15	14	12
Foreign	55	90	188	531	8	10	13	16
Corporations	127	142	175	415	19	17	12	12
Endowments and Foundations	92	102	96	267	14	12	7	8
Total	661	867	1,423	3,400	100	100	100	100

Sources: "Capital Transfusion 1982: $1.4 Billion for 54 Venture Funds," *Venture Capital Journal*, January 1983, p. 6. (Table p. 9) and "Capital Transfusion 1984: First Half Funding of $1.8 Billion for 62 Venture Firms," *Venture Capital Journal*, July 1984, p. 7. (Table p. 10).

the single largest venture capital investor from 1981 to 1983 was the Hillman Company of Pittsburgh with combined disbursements of over $282 million.[2] The size of the Hillman pool of capital is not available; it is entirely family owned.

Venture Capitalists

Venture capitalists are concentrated in the Northeast and on the West Coast, with small pockets of venture capital in the Midwest and Southwest. Table 3-2 shows the geographic distribution of venture capital resources by region for the entire industry for 1977 and 1982. It indicates that the concentration of venture capitalist dollars and firms has remained in the Northeast and the West Coast. Of the $3.4 billion raised by private independent partnerships in 1983, 52 percent went to the Northeast region, 30 percent went to the West Coast, and the remainder was split fairly evenly among the Midwest, Southeast, and Southwest.[3]

Within these regions, venture capital is heavily concentrated in four states: New York, California, Massachusetts, and Illinois. The presence of major financial centers causes large concentrations of capital in these states. Connecticut has recently emerged as a venture capital center as well. Due perhaps to its proximity to New York City and Boston, Connecticut attracted 9.2 percent of venture capital commitments to partnerships in 1983. Cities with large venture capital resource pools include Minneapolis, New York City, San Francisco, Boston, Chicago, Dallas, and Houston. The distribution of venture capital dollars and firms by state is given in table 3-3. Also illustrated in table 3-3 is the fact that, while the total pool of venture capital resources in each state has risen significantly since 1977, the increase has been proportional, with Illinois and Texas increasing by the greatest amount in percentage terms.

The empirical concentration of venture capital commitments in the Northeast has subsided somewhat, however, because of unprecedented capital infusions into California venture pools from 1981 to 1982. Nevertheless, the Northeast remains the dominant locale for venture capital resources and contains the country's largest fund, a $341 million venture pool managed by Warbug, Pincus Capital Corporation, plus four other funds whose capitalizations exceed $100 million. There are six other mega-funds: five in California and one in Baltimore. Table 3-4 shows the distribution of capital commitments among the 15 largest states for 1981 to 1983.

Venture capitalists do not necessarily invest at the location where their head offices are based; many firms have more than one office. For this reason, venture capitalists' disbursement activities are more widely distributed than the geographic distribution of capital resources might suggest. The geographic distribution of the individual venture capitalist in 1982 is shown in table 3-5.

Table 3–2
Geographic Distribution of Capital Resources by Regions, 1977 and 1983

	Capital (millions of dollars)				Firms			
	1977	Percent of Total	1983	Percent of Total	1977	Percent of Total	1983	Percent of Total
Northeast[a]	1,391	55	5,538	46	112	47	189	35
Southeast[b]	95	4	547	5	19	8	37	7
Midwest/Plains[c]	398	16	1,317	11	38	16	70	13
Southwest/Rockies[d]	113	4	759	6	24	10	82	15
West Coast[e]	524	21	3,915	32	44	19	159	30
Total	2,521	100	12,076	100	237	100	537	100

Source: "Venture Capital Industry Resources," *Venture Capital Journal*, July 1984, p. 4. (Table p. 5).

[a]CT, DE, MA, ME, NH, NJ, NY, PA, RI, VT.
[b]AL, DC, FL, GA, MD, MS, NC, SC, TN, VA, WV.
[c]IL, IN, IA, KS, KY, MI, MN, MO, NE, ND, OH, SD, WI.
[d]AR, AZ, CO, ID, LA, MT, NM, NV, OK, TX, UT, WY.
[e]CA, OR, WA.

Table 3-3
Distribution of Capital Resources by Leading States, 1977 and 1983

	Capital (millions of dollars)				Firms			
	1977	Percent of Total	1983	Percent of Total	1977	Percent of Total	1983	Percent of Total
California	524	21	3,656	30	44	19	142	26
New York	718	28	2,559	21	56	24	89	17
Massachusetts	334	13	1,549	13	28	12	45	8
Illinois	225	10	715	6	14	6	18	3
Connecticut	89	4	683	6	10	4	17	3
Texas	83	3	473	4	14	6	45	8

Source: "Venture Capital Industry Resources," *Venture Capital Journal*, July 1984, p. 4. (Table p. 5).

Table 3–4
Distribution of Capital Commitments, 1981 to 1983 (Independent Private Partnerships Only)

State	Total Capital Committed (millions of dollars)			Percent of Total Capital Committed		
	1981	1982	1983	1981	1982	1983
California	312.0	516.0	951.9	36.0	36.3	27.4
New York	115.7	334.0	952.0	13.4	23.5	27.4
Massachusetts	71.9	303.9	459.5	8.3	21.3	13.2
Illinois	38.0	19.1	35.1	4.4	1.3	1.0
New Jersey	23.0	46.7	na	2.6	3.3	na
Rhode Island	—	44.2	na	—	3.1	na
Connecticut	115.3	43.1	320.0	13.3	3.0	9.2
Colorado	—	39.4	na	—	2.8	na
Maryland	44.0	25.9	133.7	5.1	1.8	3.9
Virginia	—	15.0	na	—	1.1	na
Texas	50.9	na	126.4	5.9	na	3.6
Washington	36.5	na	109.3	4.2	na	3.2
Ohio	35.5	na	na	4.1	na	na
Iowa	20.0	na	na	2.3	na	na
Minnesota	3.8	na	123.0	0.4	na	3.5
Not Allocated	—	35.7	264.6	—	2.5	7.6
Total	866.6	1,423.0	3,475.5	100.0	100.0	100.0

Source: Capital Transfusion 1983: Transformation to an $11.5 Billion Venture Capital Pool; $3.4 Billion for 87 Private Venture Funds," *Venture Capital Journal*, January 1984, p. 6. (Table p. 11).

Table 3-5
Distribution of Individual Venture Capitalists by Geographic Location

Location	Percent of Venture Capitalists
CA	20.7
NY	19.1
MA	9.6
IL	9.1
CT	6.0
TX	4.2
OH	3.1
MN	2.9
Other	25.3

Source: David A. Silver, *Who's Who in Venture Capital,* (New York: Competere Group, 1982).

The differences between tables 3-5 and 3-3 show that while venture capital funds are committed to major financial centers, venture capitalists endeavor to distribute their attention geographically. This practice is an important factor in policy making for national and regional economic development.

The distribution of venture capital among industry portions can also be identified by employing the following definitions.

1. *Independent private partnerships*—includes venture capital partnerships and affiliated SBICs.
2. *Corporate-financial*—includes venture capital subsidiaries and affiliates of banks and insurance companies, their affiliated SBICs and publicly held venture capital firms.
3. *Corporate-industrial*—includes venture capital subsidiaries and affiliates of industrial corporations and their affiliated SBICs.
4. *Other venture capital SBICs*—includes unaffiliated, privately held venture capital related SBICs and publicly held venture capital SBICs.[4]

Details of the resource distribution among industry segments are given in table 3-6. This table makes clear that the emerging form of venture capital is now the independent private partnership. This industry segment controlled 66 percent of industry capital resources at year end 1983, up from 38 percent of capital in 1977. In dollar volume, independent private partnerships increased by eightfold their resources between 1977 and year end 1983. As shown by table 3-7, however, the absolute number of venture capital professionals did not increase as rapidly.

Professional Venture Capital Experience

On average, venture capital industry professionals managed 55 percent more capital per professional in 1983 than in 1977, as shown in table 3-7. The rapid

Table 3-6
Total Resources by Industry Category, 1977 and 1983

	Capital (millions of dollars)			Firms			Professionals		
	1977	*1983*	*Percent Increase*	*1977*	*1983*	*Percent Increase*	*1977*	*1983*	*Percent Increase*
Independent private	950	8,486	793	105	233	122	249	890	257
Corporate financial	913	1,580	73	36	44	22	119	185	55
Corporate industrial	268	1,289	381	30	34	13	67	100	49
Other venture capital SBICs	390	721	85	66	137	108	162	319	97
Total	2,521	12,076	379	237	448	89	597	1,494	150

Source: "Venture Capital Industry Resources," *Venture Capital Journal*, July 1984, p. 4.

Table 3-7
Growth of Resources by Firms and Professionals, 1977 and 1983
(by millions of dollars)

	Average Capital/Firm			Median Size	Average Capital/Professional		
	1977	*1983*	*Percent Increase*	*1983*	*1977*	*1983*	*Percent Increase*
Independent private	9.0	36.4	304	18.0	3.8	9.5	150
Corporate financial	25.4	35.9	41	14.5	7.7	8.5	10
Corporate industrial	8.9	37.9	326	10.0	4.0	12.9	223
Other SBICs	5.9	5.3	(10)	2.0	2.4	2.3	(4)
Total industry	10.6	27.0	155	10.0	4.2	8.1	93

Source: "Venture Capital Industry Resources," *Venture Capital Journal*, July 1984, p. 4.

growth of firms in the venture capital industry has depleted the availability of experienced venture capitalists. Hence, more general partners are founding new firms without the benefit of having experienced a full venture capital cycle—investment stage, growth stage, and liquidation stage. Of 61 new partnerships formed between 1977 and 1982 (as opposed to follow-on partnerships, where partners in existing firms raise new capital), partnerships with at least one general partner with 10 years' experience received 89 percent of the capital. Individual general partners, however, had less venture capital experience as illustrated in figure 3-1. In 1983 the level of general partners' experience in all funds (including follow-on funds) dropped significantly. Of 87 partnerships formed, only 45 percent had a general partner with over 10 years' experience; these partnerships attracted 65 percent of commitments to independent private partnerships.

Approximately 60 percent of venture capital during the period 1977 through 1983 went not to new partnerships, however, but to follow-on partnerships. Yearly distribution of capital resources to new and follow-on funds is provided in table 3-8.

Professional Venture Capital Education

Professionals in the venture capital industry are highly educated, with a median of one graduate degree, and sometimes as many as three postbaccalaureate degrees. Of the 451 venture capitalists listed in *Who's Who in Ven-*

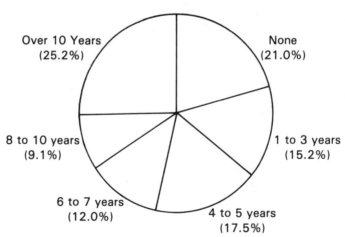

Source: "Venture Capital, The Growth of An Industry 1977-1982." *Venture Capital Journal,* October 1982, p. 8.

Figure 3-1. New Partnership Formation: Years of General Partners' Experience

Table 3-8
Formation of New and Follow-On Partnerships, 1977 to 1983, by
Number and Dollar Resources

	New		Follow-On		Total	
	Number	Resources ($ millions)	Number	Resources ($ millions)	Number	Resources ($ millions)
1977	2	20	—	—	2	20
1978	5	66	8	150	13	216
1979	7	87	7	83	14	170
1980	10	243	12	418	22	661
1981	24	389	13	477	37	866
1982	36	795	18	628	54	1423
1983	41	1119	46	2210	87	3400
Total	125	2719	104	3966	229	6756

Source: "The Growth of an Industry, Venture Capital 1977–1982," *Venture Capital Journal,* October 1982, p. 10 and "Capital Transfusion 1983," *Venture Capital Journal,* January 1984, p. 6.

ture Capital, 21 percent have received at least one degree, either college or graduate, from Harvard University. Venture capitalists hold, on average, three directorships in portfolio companies. (Refer to figures 3–2 and 3–3).

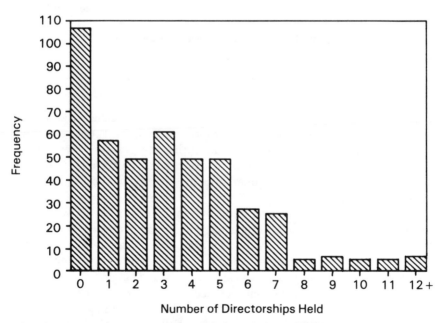

Source: Aggregated from David A. Silver, *Who's Who in Venture Capital* (New York: Competere Group, 1982). Reprinted with permission.

Figure 3–2. Venture Capitalists: Directorships Held

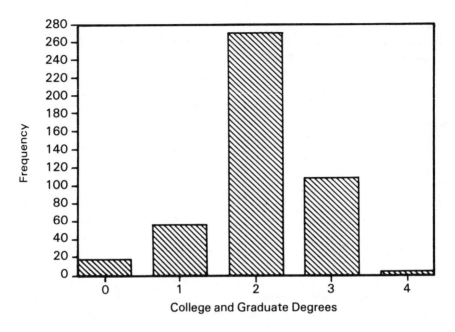

Source: Aggregated from David A. Silver, *Who's Who in Venture Capital* (New York: Competere Group, 1982). Reprinted with permission.

Figure 3-3. Venture Capitalist Education

Entrepreneurs

Disbursements of venture capital to entrepreneurs have reached record levels in recent years, as shown in figure 3-4. Indeed, over the past four years more venture capital has been disbursed than during the previous twenty years combined, and total disbursements have grown each year since 1975. In 1983 alone, more than $2.8 billion dollars was invested by venture capitalists in portfolio companies.

Statistics show an increasing trend by venture capitalists to weigh their investments toward expansion financing, when measured in terms of dollar disbursements. A 1984 study by the *Venture Capital Journal* shows that for 1983 55 percent of the estimated $2.8 billion of disbursements went to expansion stage financing, 33 percent to early-stage financing, and the remaining 10 percent went to leverage buyouts and acquisitions. The relative percentage of funds allocated by venture capitalists to early-stage funding had dropped significantly in each of the previous two years, falling from 42 percent in 1981 to 39 percent in 1982 and finally to 33 percent in 1983 (see table 3-9). One should be careful of drawing conclusions from this increasing concentration

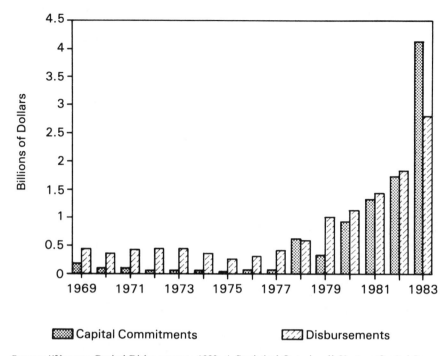

Capital Commitments   **Disbursements**

Source: "Venture Capital Disbursements 1982: A Statistical Overview," *Venture Capital Journal,* June 1983, p. 7, and "Venture Capitalists Invest $2.8 Billion in 1983, a 56% Increase Over 1982," *Venture Capital Journal,* May 1984, p. 7.

Figure 3–4. U.S. Venture Capital Industry: Disbursements and Commitments 1969–1983

in areas other than early stage financings; financing is affected by such diverse economic factors as interest rates, stock-market levels, and capital gains taxes. *Venture Capital Journal,* however, notes that there exists a "growing focus by specialized funds and direct investment by passive institutional investors in later stage and bridge financing in anticipation of public offerings."[5] There are concerns among venture capitalists that the entry of investors who are unfamiliar with the rigors of the industry will impair the optimal development of venture-backed organizations. These concerns involve the proper development of a firm in its role as a contributing economic entity.

Venture capitalists face a very high-risk/high-reward environment when they invest in emerging companies. Their commitment to an investee company, therefore, extends beyond financing and into management responsibilities; venture capitalists are trusted consultants to their portfolio companies. There exists a mutual incentive to position a company for its initial

Table 3-9
Disbursements by Financing Stage, 1981 to 1983

	Percent of Number of Financings			Percent of Dollar Amount Invested			Average Size of Financing ($ thousands)		
	1981	1982	1983	1981	1982	1983	1981	1982	1983
Early Stage									
Seed	4	5	6	2	2	3	750	800	1,300
Startup	23	19	16	22	15	11	1,850	1,550	2,000
Other Early Stage	18	21	21	18	22	19	1,850	2,000	2,700
Total Early Stage	45	45	43	42	39	33	1,750	1,700	2,300
Expansion Stage									
Second Stage	27	25	29	28	30	35	2,000	2,400	3,850
Later Stage	15	19	19	16	21	20	2,050	2,250	3,200
Total Expansion	42	44	48	44	51	55	2,000	2,300	3,650
Other (leveraged buy-outs, secondaries and acquisitions)	13	11	9	14	10	12	2,000	1,900	4,250
Total	100	100	100	100	100	100			

Source: "Venture Capital Disbursements 1982: A Statistical Overview," *Venture Capital Journal*, June 1983, p. 7 and "Venture Capitalists Invest $2.8 Billion in 1983," *Venture Capital Journal*, May 1984, p. 7.

public offering. Venture capital firms offer two advantages to the investee company that other investment organizations do not possess: (1) the investment of time and capital to protect; and (2) the managerial expertise to render.

Venture capital has been used primarily to fund entrepreneurs interested in high-technology ventures. Table 3-10, which details the distribution of venture capital among industries, clearly shows the high-technology tendency of venture capitalists.

The bent of venture capitalists toward technology seems to be accelerating. From a database kept by the IC^2 Institute at the University of Texas at Austin, which includes only giant capital venture resource pools (paid-in capital of $100 million or more) and which concentrates on early stage financing, there is evidence that investments in high technology areas will increase. This conclusion is drawn from two premises. The first premise is that start-up financings are in a general sense leading indicators of expansion financing. Furthermore, expansion financing needs are on average 59 percent larger than start-up financings. The second premise is that the largest firms in the industry, because of the volume of investment activity in which they engage, will be the first to identify leading technologies; therefore, their investments will set standards for others in the industry. The disbursements by industry of 15 giant venture capital funds for 1981–1983 are illustrated in table 3-11.

As shown by table 3-11, computer-related businesses, when software and semiconductors are included, account for 54 percent of all the early stage disbursements in the IC^2 database. When other high technology industries

Table 3-10
Disbursements by Industry, 1981 to 1983

	Percent of Number of Companies Financed			Percent of Dollar Amount Invested		
	1981	*1982*	*1983*	*1981*	*1982*	*1983*
Communications	12	10	12	11	10	13
Computer Related	29	37	40	30	43	46
Other Electronics	13	11	10	12	13	10
Genetic Engineering	5	3	3	7	3	3
Medical/Health Related	7	8	11	6	7	9
Energy	6	6	3	10	6	3
Industrial Automation	6	5	3	4	3	2
Industrial Products	6	5	3	5	4	2
Consumer Related	5	6	7	5	5	7
Other	11	9	8	10	6	5

Source: Venture Capital Disbursements, 1982: A Statistical Overview," *Venture Capital Journal,* June 1983, p. 7 and "Venture Capitalists Invest $2.8 Billion in 1983," *Venture Capital Journal,* May 1984, p. 7.

Table 3–11
Early Disbursements by Giant Venture Capital Firms,[a] by Industry,
1981 to 1983

Industry	Percent of Total Dollar Amount Invested
Communications	5.3
Computer Related	39.7
Other Electronics (semiconductors)	6.7
Genetic Engineering	6.0
Medical/Health Related	7.0
Energy (oil & gas)	12.5
Industrial Automation (robotics)	8.4
Consumer Related	1.4
Software	7.6
Other	5.4
Total	100

Source: IC^2 Institute database, The University of Texas at Austin.
[a]Partnerships with paid-in capital in excess of $100 million.

are added, including communications, genetic engineering, and industrial automation, the total reaches 73.3 percent. This figure is compared to 68 percent for the years 1981–1982 for all venture capital firms and all stages of financing as shown in table 3–10. The IC^2 database has proved a useful indicator of trends within the venture capital industry, as 75 percent of venture funds for the 1982–1983 period were invested in high technology industries. The IC^2 database also allows one to monitor the individual states in which venture capitalists are investing. The percentage of disbursements to selected states over the 1981–1982 period is given in table 3–12. California, Massachusetts, and Texas are the dominant states for disbursed venture capital. Table 3–12 also shows the percentage of 1981–1982 capital commitments by state, which provides for a comparison of the sources and disbursements of that capital. This comparison is diagramatically presented in figure 3–5.

States receiving significantly more disbursements than commitments, indicating out-of-state capital infusions, include Colorado, Florida, Georgia, Minnesota, Pennsylvania, Texas, and Virginia. Texas' large share of venture capital disbursements is directly attributable to energy investments, most of which occurred during the 1981 post-decontrol oil boom. New York and Connecticut are the two states with significantly greater commitments than disbursements, a fact attributable to the large concentrations of financial institutions in these states.

Table 3–12
Sources and Uses of Venture Capital, by State, 1981–1982
(percent of total)

	Disbursements	*Commitments*
California	36	37
Colorado	4	2
Connecticut	2	7
Florida	1	0
Georgia	2	0
Illinois	3	2
Maryland	2	3
Massachusetts	16	16
Minnesota	2	0
New Jersey	4	3
New York	5	20
Pennsylvania	2	0
Texas	12	2
Virginia	3	1
Other	6	7

Source: IC^2 Institute database, The University of Texas at Austin.

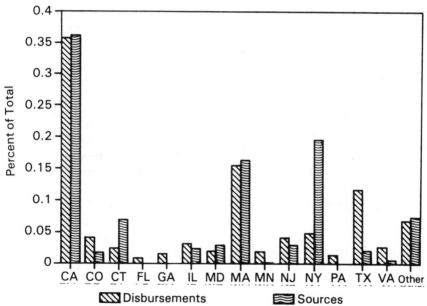

Source: IC^2 Institute database, The University of Texas at Austin.

Figure 3–5. Sources and Uses of Venture Capital: Distribution by State, 1981–1982

The Federal Government

Although there are many factors which affect the sources and disbursements of venture capital, including factors in the economic, political, technological, and psychological areas, to date the single most pervasive element which influences the venture capital process is the regulatory environment set by the federal government. The two tools which the government uses to influence the venture capital process are taxation and regulatory restrictions.

Tax policies can affect the venture capital process in a variety of ways. Tax policies directly affect both the supply of venture capital, such as pension funds and individual investors, as well as the demand for venture capital by entrepreneurs.

Sources of venture capital, that is, investors and institutions that place their funds with a venture capital partnership, have less of an incentive to invest in venture capital when capital gains taxes are high. Capital gains taxes take such a large portion of profits that investors turn to lower-risk assets with short time horizons when capital gains taxes are high. High taxes on other specific venture capital instruments, such as stock options, also can have a negative impact on the venture capital process as a whole.

The relationship between taxes and venture capital has some empirical foundations. Figure 3-4 shows the decline in venture capital commitments following the 1969 increase in capital gains taxes, from over $200 million in 1969 to about $10 million in 1975, and the explosion of commitments following the 1978 reduction in capital gains taxes, from under $100 million in 1977 to over $600 million in 1978. In 1981, further reduction of capital gains taxes helped spur capital commitments to new highs. Other factors influencing venture capital commitments include the market for initial public offerings, pension fund and insurance company regulations, and the tax treatment of warrants, convertible debentures, and other financial instruments.

Regulatory policies directly affect investors in the venture capital process. For example, in 1979, the Department of Labor published a proposed regulation change in the Federal Register for pension fund participation in venture capital investments. Though the intent of the legislation was to increase pension fund participation in venture capital pools, the legal counsel of many pension funds interpreted the legislation as creating personal fiduciary responsibility for the pension trust fund manager. As a result, many pension funds decreased their involvement in venture capital; the capital commitments fell accordingly.

Users of venture capital are also affected by governmental policies. Entrepreneurs, for example, had a more difficult time attracting venture capital during the 1969–1977 period because they found venture capital was scarce. Such a condition can stunt entrepreneurial activity. When financial incentives to entrepreneurs are substantially reduced, it is hard to attract proper management for emerging firms. Talented managers who are in salaried positions with a career-oriented job have less of an incentive to abandon their secure jobs for highly risky endeavors; the marginal difference between existing salaries and bonuses versus the potential of highly taxed capital gains and stock options is insufficient to compensate for such a risky career move.

Venture capitalists are also affected by the regulatory environment imposed on them by government. During periods of high capital gains taxes, venture capitalists shift their orientation from starting new businesses and other long-term commitments to buying out existing enterprises or making short-term liquid investments to reduce risks. The lack of venture capital commitments during these periods also diminishes the number of new entrants into the industry, thereby also decreasing apprenticeship opportunities for new venture capitalists. This training is felt by many to constitute a necessary foundation for industry soundness. This concern is especially poignant in light of the recent surge in venture capital investments. The barrier facing a venture capitalist in an endeavor to build a successful firm is no longer how much money can be raised, but rather, how many entrepreneurial firms one can help manage. Hence, consistency of governmental regulation is an important factor which affects the venture capitalist.

Other causal factors which have an impact on the venture capitalist's working environment are more difficult to identify and assess. It is not clear from available data, for example, how regulation on a state level affects the venture capital process as a whole. Such regulation, however, does provide the environment for many short-term decisions, such as the selection of the state in which to base home offices, research development laboratories, and manufacturing operations. Another example of the difficulty of assessing working environment factors is the state of technological progress. Despite the fact that technology is a primary driver of successful venture capital, the broad sweep of such an assessment makes either a qualitative or quantitative analysis for working purposes almost impossible. Nevertheless, such factors as governmental regulation on the state level and technological trends in general are important to the venture capital working environment and need to be recognized.

A recent study by the General Accounting Office (GAO) affirmed the significant impact that government regulations have on the venture capital industry.[6] While studying the impact of government regulation, the GAO also analyzed the benefits the industry provides society. The GAO studied a sample of 207 firms which were founded during the 1970s and which subsequently went public. An economic-benefit analysis was performed using the statistics of 72 companies in this sample. With an aggregate investment by venture capitalists of $209 million, these companies provided the following aggregate economic benefits during the 1970s:

1. aggregate sales in 1979 alone of $6 billion which, in the latter five years (1974–1979), were growing at an annual rate of 33 percent,
2. an estimated 130,000 jobs,
3. over $100 million in corporate tax revenues,
4. $350 million in employee tax revenues, and
5. $900 million in export sales.

By 1989, the GAO estimates that venture-backed companies could generate the following amounts:

1. $3 billion to $7.6 billion in corporate taxes,
2. $8 billion to $22.7 billion in employee taxes,
3. $26 billion to $81.9 billion in export sales, and
4. 522,000 to 2,244,000 jobs.

Illustrated in figure 3–6 are the GAO's projections for 1989. In addition, the GAO noted that these venture-backed firms brought to market primarily productivity-enhancing technology products. This indicates that venture capital firms improve not only the stability and productivity of the firms they

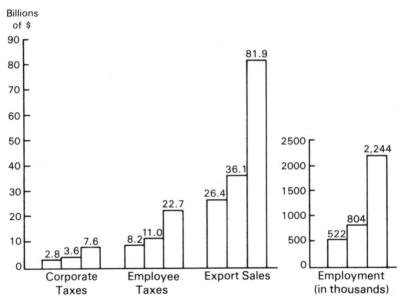

Source: U.S. General Accounting Office, *Government-Industry Cooperation Can Enhance the Venture Capital Process,* GAO/AMFD–82–35, August 12, 1982, p. 15.

Figure 3–6. Projected Venture Capital Benefits for 1989: Medium and High Scenarios

finance, but also the stability and productivity of firms in various other segments of the economy. The extent to which venture capital investment has an impact on other segments of the economy is impressive. The GAO estimates that for every $1,000 of venture capital invested in the 1970s, $40,000 to $54,000 worth of productivity-enhancing products and services will be sold during the 1980s. The GAO report demonstrates the truly sensitive and dynamic nature of the venture capital investment process.

Notes

1. "Venture Capitalists Invest $2.8 Billion in 1983," *Venture Capital Journal,* May 1984, p. 7.

2. "The Venture Capital 100," *Venture,* June issues, 1982–1984.

3. "Venture Capitalists Invest," p. 12.

4. "The Growth of an Industry: Venture Capital 1977–1982," *Venture Capital Journal,* October 1982, p. 8.

5. "Venture Capital Disbursements 1982, A Statistical Overview," *Venture Capital Journal,* June 1983, p. 7.

6. U.S. General Accounting Office, *Government-Industry Cooperation Can Enhance the Venture Capital Process,* GAO/AMFD-83-35, August 12, 1982, p. 15.

4

New Initiatives in Venture Capital: State-Created Venture Capital Pools and Incubators

T hus far, this book has focused on venture capital that falls into definable segments. These segments have been delineated primarily through each segment's distinct sources of funds, tax status, profit goals, and regulatory restrictions. With the exception of R&D partnerships, the formation and practices of industry segments have been relatively consistent for over twenty years. By any standards, the venture capital industry as a whole has been an unqualified success, returning extraordinary profits to its investors, expanding national productivity, creating jobs, and expanding the tax base. It is important to note, however, that venture capital alone does not cause these benefits; rather, entrepreneurship is the real driver behind these positive effects. In other words, venture capital is a catalyst. It is, in fact, the primary institutionalized mechanism to facilitate entrepreneurship in today's economy.

As a facilitator, the venture capital industry aids the entrepreneurial process in two distinct ways: with financial resources and with managerial assistance. The financial input removes a critical bottleneck to the development of entrepreneurial talent and the subsequent commercialization of the entrepreneur's product or service. Managerial assistance, a term which encompasses advice given in such areas as financial services, accounting, personnel management, marketing, and engineering services, provides support to the natural abilities of the entrepreneur. While these services cannot replace the entrepreneur, they can multiply his natural abilities.

Traditional venture capital institutions recognize the creative forces inherent in entrepreneurship. Their incentive to aid the entrepreneurial process is a share of the potential profit, which historically has been a compounded 25–40 percent return on investment. Besides the high return on investment, venture-backed entrepreneurship has secondary benefits, notably employment, tax revenues, and foreign trade. Just as traditional venture capital institutions were formed to exploit the profit opportunities in entrepreneurship, so have other institutionalized entities formed in order to exploit venture capital's secondary benefits. Specifically, various leading states have organized venture capital funds to assist job creation. Universities and local communities have also organized "new business incubators" whose goals, though mixed, emphasize economic development, job creation, and commercialization of newer technologies.

State Venture Capital Funds

State-government-sponsored venture capital programs have increased dramatically in size and numbers since 1980. Prior to 1980, only Connecticut, Massachusetts, and Wyoming had state-funded venture capital-type funds. Since 1980, six additional states have established venture capital funds. The size of the funds, funding sources, investment parameters, and investment recovery methods vary among states. Table 4-1 illustrates the differences in funding sources, investment parameters, and investment instruments between the various states' venture funds.

Funding for state-sponsored venture capital comes primarily from the sponsoring state's treasury. Connecticut and New Mexico have venture funds whose capital comes exclusively from the state government. Other states complement their state funds with federal funds: New York and Massachusetts are an example of this funding strategy. Michigan and Georgia supplement their venture capital funds with private capital. Other states such as Indiana, Iowa, Minnesota, and Wyoming fund their venture pools with private capital by granting tax incentives to private investors. The Massachusetts Capital Resource Corporation (MCRC) is also privately funded, but is unique in that its investors, Massachusetts-based life insurance companies, are required to invest in the fund by punitive state taxes. If the life insurance companies do not meet quotas set by the legislature in terms of dollars invested and jobs created, then special taxes are imposed. In the first three years of this legislated equity allocation, MCRC invested $54 million.[1]

Many state-sponsored venture capital funds are restricted in their investment activity by either the fund's charter or by legislation. Generally, states restrict a fund's investment orientation to areas where there are perceived shortages of private venture capital; early stage financings are the usual target area. Early stage financings are often slighted by private venture capitalists due to the large administrative expenses associated with such financings, expenses which include time—often the venture capitalist's most scarce resource. States whose venture capital funds specialize in this type of financing are Connecticut, Georgia, Iowa, Minnesota, and New Mexico. Conversely, New York and Massachusetts funds specialize in high technology. Indiana's Corporation for Innovation Development is unique in that it does not make direct venture capital financings, but rather invests in Indiana-based SBICs and venture capital pools. Massachusetts' Community Development Finance Corporation also does not make direct investments, but channels its investments through a community development corporation.

Table 4-1
Summary of Selected State Venture Capital Pools

State Venture Capital Fund and Fund Name	Year Organized	Total Funding (millions of dollars)	Funding Source	Investment Parameters	Investment Instruments
Connecticut Connecticut Product Development Corp.	1975	10	State	Product development	Royalty payment
Georgia Advanced Technology Development Fund	1980	10	50% State 50% Private	Seed financing	Equity participation
Indiana Corporation for Innovation Development	1981	10	Equity sale w/tax deduction	Direct or indirect financing	Equity participation
Iowa Iowa Fund	1983	15	Equity sale w/tax deduction	Start-up	Equity participation
Massachusetts Mass. Capital Resource Corp.	1978	54	Private, with state incentives	Companies with bad credit ratings	Equity participation
Mass. Technology Development Corp.	1978	3.4	State and Federal funds	Mass.-based high tech	Debt and equity participation
Community Development Finance Corporation	1975	10	Bond sale	Investments thru community dev. corps	Debt and equity participation
Michigan Michigan Investment Fund	1983	60	State pension fund, private	60% Michigan	Equity participation
Minnesota Minnesota Seed Capital Fund	1982	5	Private	Early stage in Minnesota	Equity participation
New Mexico Business Development Corporation	1983	1.8	State	Small business	Debt
New York Corporation for Innovation Development	1981	2	State and Federal funds	High technology	Debt and Equity participation
Utah Utah Innovation Center	1983	1.5	State	High technology	Equity participation
Wyoming Wyoming Industrial Development Corp.	1976	8	Private	None	Debt and Equity

Nearly all state venture capital pools make their investments in the form of equity financings. New Mexico, however, differs in that it makes only debt financings. The Massachusetts Technology Development Corporation makes mixed investments of debt plus equity.

University-Related Incubators

State governments, local governments, and private institutions have all begun to realize that the primary driver of technology-based business formation is neither the availability of funds nor the rate of technological advance, but rather the availability of entrepreneurial talent. Simply stated, technological innovation is driven by entrepreneurs, not by money, government or universities. Successful entrepreneurship takes a wide variety of talents. However, it is rare to find a potential entrepreneur who combines the technical expertise necessary for technological innovation with the business acumen necessary for successful product commercialization. One concept which has developed in the last five years to facilitate the development of entrepreneurial creativity and education is the incubator unit.

Incubator units are designed to assist technically-oriented entrepreneurs in developing their business skills in an environment that simultaneously stimulates technical creativity. Although incubators vary in the scope of assistance provided, there are some generic components to the incubator concept. Most incubator units are university related. After screening potential entrepreneurs, they provide low cost office and/or laboratory space, administrative services, access to library and computer facilities, skilled consultants, an inexpensive work force in the form of graduate and undergraduate students, and special contacts with bankers, venture capitalists, technologists, and government officials. In this environment an aspiring entrepreneur is free to be technologically creative since his energies can be devoted to product development and not to the rigors of obtaining financing or managing an organization. All the while, the entrepreneur is associated with other entrepreneurs facing similar barriers, an association which should, it is hoped, stimulate the entrepreneur's drive for success.

An incubator unit is not only an organization, but also a physical unit. Incubators start as a single building or group of buildings where the participating entrepreneurs can be housed and where, due to physical proximity, they will spontaneously interact. In the building there may be space for twenty or more entrepreneurs. The institution sponsoring the incubator will provide secretarial support, duplicating services, accounting services, technical editing help, computer equipment, conference space, health and other benefit packages, and access to university facilities and expertise for a nominal fee. The advantages of being on or near a university campus are numerous: library facilities, exposure to state-of-the-art technical thinking and equipment, undergraduates that form a pool of cheap and technically skilled labor, a creative environment, and potential employment as a lecturer. Companies within the incubator profit from the technical resources of the university in a variety of ways. These companies benefit from the best available talent when they need it without having to carry that high-priced talent on their payroll. And they receive the stimulus and catalytic effect associated with working alongside outstanding professionals from outside their organization.

Organizationally, incubators differ from one another due to their varying priorities; these are different because of the funding sources that support the incubator unit. Funding sources for these units include federal, state, and local governments, universities, private individuals and foundations, financial intermediaries, and corporations. Incubators can be associated with any of these funding sources to varying degrees and therefore have similar goals but different priorities. The general goals of incubators are to develop firms, often technically based, and stimulate entrepreneurship. Incubators may seek to develop jobs; create investment opportunities for college endowments; expand a tax base for local government; enhance the image of college technical programs; speed transfer of technological innovation from the academic world to industry; fill a perceived gap in venture capital financing by improving the quality of locally-based entrepreneurial talent; and build a core of indigenous companies.

Science parks often accompany the incubator unit as another link between universities and industry. Located near universities, the objective of these parks is to attract both research and development and the manufacturing facilities of established technology-based companies. Science parks, also called technology or research parks, act as a lightning rod for technology-based companies and can be an area's lure for pirating companies from out of state. Science parks also give universities a method of further benefiting from the development of firms incubated in their facilities, since these firms are prime candidates for research park tenants.

A review of selected incubators provides insights into the structure, operation, and diversity of this innovative approach to business development (see also table 4-2).

The University City Science Center (UCSC) in Philadelphia has been a prototype university-related incubator/research center for twenty years. Organized as a non-profit corporation, UCSC has 28 "shareholders," which are the major universities, colleges, and medical schools in the Philadelphia area, plus the local community development organization. UCSC is the only entirely urban research park in the United States. UCSC derives its name from the West Philadelphia neighborhood where it is located, which contains the University of Pennsylvania, Drexel University, the Philadelphia College of Pharmacy and Science, the Philadelphia General Hospital, the Veterans

Administration Hospital, the Presbyterian University of Pennsylvania Medical Center, and the city convention center. Other major academic institutions, from Villanova to Swarthmore, are within driving distance from UCSC and are also shareholders. The unique shareholder/nonprofit-institution combination is not as contradictory as it may seem, since the association is intended to increase collaboration among UCSC and its member organizations.

UCSC is composed of two groups, the Research Park Division and the Research Institutes Division. The Research Park Division is part incubator and part science park. Of the 75 companies currently housed in the Research Park, 38 started operations there. The research park assists entrepreneurs with administrative support services, affordable space and facilities, development of business plans, evaluation of ideas for products as bases for new businesses, financing, consulting services, and topical seminars. Other tenants in the Research Park are more established concerns with businesses in technology related areas. The UCSC Research Park currently has eight buildings containing 75 companies. These companies have aggregate employment of 5,225 workers, have a $110 million payroll, pay $4.7 million in wage taxes to the city, $.93 million in real estate taxes, and $2.1 million in state income taxes. UCSC has a total capital investment of $45 million in nine completed buildings with 1.1 million square feet of office space, the vast majority of which is filled by high technology firms. Plans for the Research Park Division call for a total capital investment when completed of $250 million. The envisioned park would have five million square feet of space and employ within its facilities over 20,000 persons.[2]

The Research Institutes Division of UCSC has a professional staff of 90 researchers who undertake contract research for tenant firms or other private and public sector clients. The Research Institute has over the past several years conducted over $44 million of research, either alone or in collaboration with shareholding institutions. Of the $44 million in research grants and contract research, the UCSC Research Institute has passed 25 percent of the work through to the institutions for collaborative work. The Research Institute has a definite advantage when competing with other research centers for contracts because of its flexibility in acquiring expert research collaboration from member institutions and because the research park enables space to be readily available. This research institute provides UCSC invaluable prestige in academic, industry, and research circles, and enhances its desirability as a location for both start-up and existing firms.

UCSC also reviews funds through its designation as the base for the Advanced Technology Center of Southeastern Pennsylvania under the state-sponsored Ben Franklin Partnership (BFP). The BFP assigned $10 million of legislature-authorized funds to four advanced-technology centers around

Pennsylvania. The BFP funds have attracted $28.29 million of matching funds from the private sector, foundations, and the federal government. UCSC received $2.3 million from the BFP and obtained $9.4 million in matching funds. These funds are to go to 75 projects and will support cooperative research and development centers based at UCSC, including the Center for Advanced Sensor Technologies, the Center for Human Adaptability in Space, the Center for Advanced Biomedical Technologies, and the Center for Technologies for the Handicapped.[3] The synergy of research park, advanced technology center, research institute, and incubation unit can have the potential for significant development of entrepreneurial activity.

The Western Pennsylvania Advanced Technology Center is Pittsburgh's counterpart to the University City Science Center in Philadelphia. Funded by the Ben Franklin Partnership, the center has received over $10 million for research and development. Of this money, $3.35 million came from the BFP, $1.2 million from participating universities, $1.1 million from foundations and nonprofit institutions, and $.5 million from the federal government. The center is sponsored by the University of Pittsburgh and Carnegie-Mellon University. Like the UCSC, the Western Pennsylvania Center has incubation facilities, although this is only one of its functions. The objective of the center, like that of the Ben Franklin Partnership, is to create jobs. To achieve this objective, the center has taken an integrated approach to job creation, with three distinct components. First the center sponsors joint industry/university research and development projects in the areas of robotics, biomedical technology, high-technology materials, coal, and metals. Second, the center offers assistance to entrepreneurs, small businesses, and regional industries. This function includes the provision for an incubator unit. Third, the center aids education, training, and retraining programs to meet the labor needs of its region. Since the center is cosponsored by Carnegie-Mellon University, the critical mass of technical resources is complemented by Carnegie-Mellon's Robotics Institute.[4]

Rensselaer Polytechnic Institute (RPI), a Troy, New York university, started its incubator unit in 1980. The program now has had 17 firms in its incubator unit. Currently, the firms in the incubator unit have sales of $2 million and employ over 100 people both full and part time. RPI provides entrepreneurial firms inexpensive space for operations and access to campus facilities. All transactions are on a cash basis, though RPI has accepted stock in a company as payment for rent.[5]

In a related development, the New York state legislature has established at RPI the *New York Center for Industrial Innovation.* The state will spend $30 million building the center and will lease the facilities to RPI for $600,000 per year. The funds for equipping the building will be provided by the private sector at a cost of $35 million. The thrust of the center's initial research will be directed to the application of electronics and computers to manufacturing processes and productivity improvements, including studies of robots and automated assembly. This combination of a research facility and an incubator unit makes RPI's facilities a premier location for job creation, technological innovation, and entrepreneurship.[6]

In Atlanta, the *Georgia Advanced Technology Center* (GATC) is a state-sponsored program which runs an integrated program of venture capital investment, incubation, and entrepreneurial stimulation and assistance. Started in 1980, the GATC has a consulting arm, incubation space, and a venture capital fund. Its consulting division, named the Georgia Advanced Technology Development Corporation, has a permanent staff of 12, 5 of whom have management responsibilities, with the rest being technical consultants. GATC's incubation unit has over a dozen companies currently residing in its facilities, all of which are less than three years old and which came to the incubation unit as seed or start-up companies. GATC supports these companies for no longer than three years, after which it either helps them obtain other financing sources or uses its venture capital subsidiary to fund them. The Advanced Technology Development Fund, with a $10 million capitalization, was funded in 1983 by private investors and the state of Georgia. GATC, however, leverages outside venture capital financing as much as possible by sponsoring a venture capital conference at the Georgia Tech campus. GATC screens applications from prospective entrepreneurs, grooms their business plans and presentation, and then brings in venture capitalists to review their proposals. In 1982, approximately half of the 17 entrepreneurs making presentations received venture capital funding.[7]

The *Utah Innovation Center* (UIC), based in Salt Lake City, is a private incubation facility which developed from a quasi-public organization affiliated with the University of Utah. Started in 1978 with a grant from the National Science Foundation, UIC is privately funded by individuals. Dr. Wayne Brown, the founder of UIC and its principal owner, is a former Dean of the College of Engineering at the University of Utah. He is a successful entrepreneur himself and is the guiding force behind the incubator concept in Utah. UIC operations are funded from the center's capitalization and from income from continuing operations. For cash flow, the center consults with nonincubator firms, forms R&D partnerships to carry out research at the center, leases office space in UIC buildings, and applies for government grants. UIC has been the recipient of grants from the Department of Housing and Urban Development and the Department of Health and Human Services.

Currently, UIC has 12 firms located in its incubation facilities, with another three firms under contract for consulting services only. The firms located in the incubator facility have approximately 50 employees and are mostly in the seed stage of development. UIC has nearly completed a permanent building of which it will occupy only 15 percent; the remaining space will be leased out. Although it is not a venture capital firm, UIC does take an equity position in firms located within its incubator and becomes a full business partner with the entrepreneur. In return, UIC provides all services commonly associated with incubators. Since it has a full-time staff of only eight people, it often contracts with consultants from the University of Utah and from industry sources to help incubator firms. As in other incubator units, UIC has to screen carefully its prospective entrepreneurs, most of whom come from the University of Utah.

The screening process usually employs the analytical methods used by venture capitalists, which generally means the center invests in entrepreneurs, not ideas. Because Utah has few active venture capital firms, most of the center's contacts in venture capital come from either the East or West Coast. Recently, the Utah legislature created the Utah Technology Finance Corporation, a corporation which is intended to support entrepreneurship activities in high technology. Dr. Brown is a director of this quasi-venture-capital firm, but UIC and the Utah Technology Finance Corp. are not otherwise related. UIC is now in the process of setting up incubation centers in two other Utah cities, Orem and Logan, and has acted as a consultant to other cities which are also attempting to found incubator units. The University of Utah has a research park located very near to UIC, but they are not related.[8]

One of the most recent university-related entrants to the incubator industry is Texas A&M University. Founded in January 1983 and funded in September 1983, A&M's *Institute for Ventures in New Technology* (INVENT) is a state-funded incubator headquartered at Texas A&M's Research Park. INVENT is funded with $1 million dollars for its first two years and has a building located in the university's research park with 5,000 square feet of space in which to locate its portfolio companies. INVENT provides companies with consulting in such areas as product development, business planning, market surveys, and equity funding availability. For its services, INVENT receives a share of a company's equity. It does no consulting for fees, only for equity. Consultants come from the university's faculty, and the institute has the equivalent of twelve full-time employees. INVENT was organized to stimulate industrial development, create jobs, and provide prospective tenants for the A&M research park. One potential problem, however, is that the research park will not accept manufacturing firms, while the incubator concept is specifically intended to promote manufacturing companies. In accordance with its charter, INVENT must become self-supporting within nine years.[9]

Private-Sector Incubators

Conceptually, private-sector incubators are similar to public-sector or university-related incubators. Both provide flexible office space, conference facilities, secretarial and duplication services, group insurance programs, and so forth. Both want to develop new business concepts into viable and growing companies. However, private sector incubator units differ from university-related incubator units in two distinct areas: funding source and goals. Private sector incubators are founded by and capitalized from private sources; there is no government involvement. The primary motive in founding the incubator unit is to make a profit. Other goals such as community development and job creation are subordinated to the profit motive. In this sense, private sector incubator units can apply venture capital techniques and analysis similar to those used for the various segments of the venture capital industry as described in chapter 2.

The investment strategy for incubators is different from that of most venture capital firms. It focuses on preseed and seed stage companies whereas the strategy of venture capital firms deals more with the take-off growth stages. Private incubators place no boundaries on the industries in which they will invest, but prefer technology-oriented investments. Capital gains are emphasized over dividend income, and the incubator's parent corporation distributes income to its investors on a variable basis. Further, an incubator is an ongoing concern, and does not liquidate itself after its investments mature. Rather, it distributes income, provides access to further investment in successful incubator firms, and/or reinvests the proceeds of its investment in new companies within the incubator. The incubator is taxed as a corporation, though some investment pools that function in conjunction with the incubator can be formed as partnerships. These companion investment pools are a type of venture capital pool: they liquidate at the end of a predetermined period, are formed exclusively for the purpose of investing in the incubator's tenants, and are managed by the incubator's management. When the incubator's facilities are full, there is no room for future growth. The only future investments available through the incubator unit are follow-on financings, financings of new firms that replace the incubator's business failures or successes that move on to larger facilities.

Companies within a privately sponsored incubator unit have one distinct advantage over nonprivate incubators—postincubator financing. Incubators generally take a substantial portion of a company's equity in return for services offered, and few public incubators have sufficient capitalization to make the large follow-on investments small companies require to continue their growth patterns. For companies developed by publicly sponsored incubators, venture capital can be difficult to obtain. Venture capital firms may be wary of investing in a company that has a significant portion of its equity held by a passive investor. Some venture capitalists require controlling interest in the firms in which they invest and if too large a portion of the equity is held by outside investors, they may not be able to secure control.

Venture capitalists have for years practiced a form of incubation by giving seed investments office space in spare rooms in their own offices. But only in 1976 was the first dedicated incubator unit formed. There are now a number of variations of the incubator concept. For example, Nolan Bushnell, the well-known entrepreneur who founded Atari and Pizza Time Theatres, has set up an investment pool named the Catalyst Fund. The purpose of the fund is to commercialize Bushnell's product ideas. There are only a few true private sector incubators around the country thus far. Two of these are the Technology Center and the Rubicon Group.

The *Technology Center,* which was started in 1976 in Montgomeryville, Pennsylvania, was one of the nation's first incubators, public or private. Since that first incubation center was opened, two other centers have been opened in other regions of the country, and seven others are planned by the end of 1985. In addition to the usual range of support services, the Technology Center also offers a variety of consulting services and opportunities. The "Center Champion" is responsible for helping the tenant develop business plans, marketing strategies and financing opportunities. As an experienced entrepreneur, the Center Champion is qualified to act as an expert consultant and has a variety of personal contacts to refer to as well. Furthermore, the Technology Center networks its tenants through a newsletter and directory which includes a brief profile on each company and its product or service. Another directory, which is computer-based, serves as a catalog of tenant companies, thereby providing ready access to hundreds of potential consultants, subcontractors, partners, suppliers, and customers.

Each Technology Center has a pool of capital for funding potential tenants and for participating in a national fund, the Technology Fund. The local pool of capital is typically financed primarily with local and regional capital and is designed to provide start-up or seed funding for small companies, typically in the $50,000 to $400,000 range. Investment opportunities for this fund are not limited to tenant companies, nor are tenant companies assured financing through the fund. The Center Champion is responsible for scouting opportunities for the fund and submits new proposals to the fund's management, which uses its resources in other Technology Centers to evaluate the proposal's viability. Additionally, each local fund has a share in a national fund, which invests in follow-on financings for outstanding companies supported by local funds. An investment by either the local or national fund is monitored by the Center Champion.[10]

The *Rubicon Group* is located in Austin, Texas. Like the Technology Center, Rubicon was founded by a successful entrepreneur who invested the gains from his venture in an incubator. Unlike the Technology Center, the Rubicon Group does not have one Center Champion, but rather a panel of advisors, each with a distinct expertise in the financial, marketing, legal, or

Table 4-2
Summary of Selected University-Related Incubator Units

	Georgia Advanced Technology Development Corporation	Utah Innovation Center	Institute for Ventures in New Technology	University City Science Center	Western Pennsylvania Advanced Technology Center	Rensselaer Polytechnic Institute
Location	Atlanta	Salt Lake City	College Station	Philadelphia	Pittsburgh	Troy, N.Y.
Date founded	1980	1978	1983	1964	1980	1980
Incubator size				w/Research park:		
companies	na	12	0	75	na	17
employees	na	50	0	5225	na	100
sales of companies	na	na	0		na	$2 million
office space	100,000 sq ft	na	5,000 sq ft	1,000,000 sq ft	22,000 sq ft	na
incubator staff	12	8	12	90	na	na
Founded by						
private sources	no	yes	no	yes	no	no
public sources	no	yes	yes	yes	yes	no
university related	yes	yes	yes	yes	yes	yes
Funding provided by						
federal government	no	yes	no	yes	no	no
state government	yes	no	yes	yes	yes	yes
local government	no	no	no	yes	yes	no
private sector	no	yes	no	yes	yes	no
university(ies)	yes	yes	yes	yes	yes	yes
Consulting services provided by						
university	yes	formerly	yes	yes	for hire	yes
private institute	no	yes	no	yes	yes	no
Physical location of incubator						
university grounds	yes	no	yes	no	no	yes
incubator unit owned facilities	no	yes	no	yes	no	no
rented space	no	no	no	no	yes	no

Primary goals					
profit	no	yes	yes	no	no
jobs	yes	no	yes	yes	no
industrial stimu-lation	yes	no	yes	yes	no
Related activities					
research for hire	no	no	no	yes	no
consulting	yes	yes	yes	yes	yes
research park:					
affiliated	yes	no	yes	yes	yes
located close by	no	yes	no	no	no
real estate speculation	no	yes	no	no	no
Venture capital availability					
incubator affiliated	yes	no	no	no	some
state government affiliated	yes	yes	no	no	no
private in-state	no	no	yes	yes	yes
private out-of-state	yes	yes	yes	yes	yes

technological areas. Rubicon invests only in the Austin area, although entrepreneurs from all over the country are recruited. Unlike other incubator units that own an entire building, Rubicon rents space only as the need arises.

Rubicon funds tenant companies through a pool of capital which is set up as a partnership. Each investment is established as a joint venture between the entrepreneur and the Rubicon Group's investment partnership. Rubicon typically takes from 20 percent to 60 percent of a company's equity for its investment and services. Rubicon plans a two-year turnover of all its companies. Each tenant firm within a two-year period will fail, grow large enough to make it on its own, or expand outside the incubator with follow-on financing.

Summary

Incubators have become an innovative approach to help small business in the start-up phase with reduced overhead costs, expert assistance, and financial backing. Incubator facilities have typically been organized using partitioned areas in existing buildings. New businesses can operate with a minimum of rented floor space and have access to shared services—secretarial, shipping and receiving, fabrication shops, storage, and special technical equipment. Many incubators also provide access to initially reduced-cost or free business assistance in critical areas such as marketing, finance, accounting, and business plan preparation.

Incubators have been established by a variety of organizations, including universities, private entrepreneurs, public/private partnerships, and charitable foundations, and by management organizations on a franchised basis. In most locales, there can be considerable value in the reduced overhead costs, access to specialized services and equipment that entrepreneurs could not otherwise afford, skilled and experienced business advice and assistance, and a supportive environment that arises from a number of co-located new businesses.

The growing interest in this concept and its contribution to business and economic development indicate that incubators may be applied in many communities across the United States within the next several years.

Notes

1. William Baldwin, "City Hall Discovers Venture Capital," *Forbes,* February 16, 1981.

2. Drawn from discussions with individuals at University City Science Center and organizational information packets.

3. Ibid.

4. Drawn from discussions with individuals at the Western Pennsylvania Advanced Technology Center and organizational information packets.

5. Richard Phadon, "University as Venture Capitalist," *Forbes,* December 19, 1983, p. 82.

6. National Governor's Association, "Technology and Growth: State Initiatives in Technological Innovation," draft final report of the Task Force on Technological Innovation, July 1983, p. 81.

7. Laton McCartney, "Academia, Inc.," *Datamation,* March 1983, p. 116; and organizational information packets from the Georgia Advanced Technology Center.

8. Drawn from discussions with individuals at the Utah Innovation Center and organizational information packets.

9. W. Arthur Porter, "A Description of the Purpose of Goals of the Institute for Venturers in New Technology (INVENT)," *Technology Venturing Databook,* IC^2 Institute, The University of Texas at Austin, 1984, p. 341.

10. Loren Schultz, "The Technology Center Concept," *New Business Incubators,* IC^2 Institute, The University of Texas at Austin, 1984, p. 4.

5
Foreign Venture Capital

T he institutionalization of venture capital is a phenomenon that originated in the United States. Its roots are traceable partially to the private sector, where The American Research and Development Corporation initiated operations in 1946, and partially to the public sector, the federal government, whose Small Business Act of 1958 propelled venture capital to industrial status. The development of venture capital in the United States is attributable to a critical mass of entrepreneurial talent with both technical and financial expertise, and to the proper environment necessary for such an industry to exist.

Venture capital in foreign countries is a more recent phenomenon than in the United States. The lag in development of foreign venture capital is related to the many factors whose synergy is necessary for venture capital to flourish. Since venture capital is most often defined in terms of the U.S. experience, it is first necessary to understand the framework in the United States which enables venture capital in this country to prosper before examining venture capital as it is practiced abroad.

The Venture Capital Framework in the United States

As defined in chapter 1, there are four elements which form the cornerstones of the venture capital industry. They are:

1. investors,
2. venture capitalists,
3. entrepreneurs, and
4. government.

The government, whether federal, state, or local, is an important element of the venture capital process. Its implied sponsorship is the first variable necessary to the development of a venture capital industry. Through its regulatory and taxation powers, the government can either create or remove the incentives which draw the potential participants of the venture capital process together. These incentives enable venture capital participants to develop their investments without significant governmental interference in the form of either regulatory constraints or tax burden.

For investors in the venture capital process, this means that the government cannot take away the unique profit incentives which make venture capital an attractive investment. In the United States, the primary incentive which makes venture capital a viable investment alternative is the favorable tax treatment of profits as long-term capital gains. Profits classified as long-term capital gains are taxed at a 20 percent rate, as compared to the tax on ordinary income, which can be as high as 50 percent. The important factor in this incentive format is that long-term profits are greater than short-term profits by a sufficiently large amount to compensate investors for the increased risk. When the combination of taxes enhances this view of long-term capital gains, then government helps to create a favorable environment for investors to place their money with venture capitalists.

Regulatory constraints can also have an impact on venture investors. Institutional investors are regulated by governments, a fact significant to the venture capital process because of the large involvement of pension funds in venture capital. In the United States, for example, venture capital has not until recently been considered an appropriate investment for certain pension funds because of its perceived high risk. One factor which changed this perception has been the desire of state governments to stimulate small business investment in their states. To achieve this goal, state pension funds have been legislatively directed to invest in venture capital pools whose investment orientation is in that state. Other factors which have contributed to the increased involvement by pension funds in venture capital include (1) the better understanding of the venture capital process by pension fund managers due to the increased empirical evidence of venture capital's viability as an investment vehicle, and (2) the acceptance by the federal government of venture capital as a legitimate institutional investment alternative.

The individual venture capitalist is affected directly and indirectly by the regulatory and taxation policies of the government. This generalization does not apply, of course, to those forms of venture capital created by legislative fiat such as business development companies or small business investment companies since these institutions exist only because of government regulations. The venture capitalist's existence is a result of the availability of funding and investment opportunities. Areas where the federal government can significantly help or hinder the venture capitalist's efforts include the tax status of the limited partnership and the regulations surrounding an initial public offering. The limited partnership is the vehicle which enables the investor to take advantage of his investment incentive; the initial public offering is the vehicle which enables the venture capitalist to provide his pool liquidity. European venture capitalists do not have the opportunity to exploit R&D limited partnerships, for example, because of prohibitive taxes and regulatory laws governing the formation and marketing of such partnerships.

A public market for venture-capital-backed securities is imperative to venture capital investment. In the United States, the most important incentive for investment in a venture capital partnership is the taxation of profits as long-term capital gains rather than as ordinary income. Without a public market for venture-backed companies, investors would not have sufficient liquidity to obtain capital gains, and would therefore lose the incentive to invest in venture capital. Government can affect a public market either favorably or unfavorably through its regulations. The proper ingredients for a public market that inspires investor confidence and liquidity include the following variables:

1. full disclosure laws,
2. rules requiring sufficient shares be issued to ensure liquidity,
3. professional brokers to provide market confidence, depth and breadth, and
4. policing of market abnormalities.

Another issue which has an impact on the efficient functioning of the venture capital process is the training of the individual venture capitalist. In this highly specialized profession, it is imperative that the venture capitalist have experience in each of the phases of a partnership's cycle. In a partnership's life, generally seven to ten years, there are three distinct phases: the investment phase, the development phase, and the liquidation phase. These phases overlap and are generally two to three years in length. Each phase requires distinct talents and experience on the part of the venture capitalist. Hence, venture capital is one of the few remaining areas where the apprenticeship system is still actively used. This signifies that the expansion of venture capital (after the environment is changed in a manner favorable to venture capital) requires a minimum lag time of seven years to effectuate. This time lag in training future venture capitalists is an important bottleneck to consider in the development of a venture capital industry.

Although the availability of entrepreneurs is not directly affected by the regulatory environment, entrepreneurs are influenced by perceived changes in the market. A perceived shortage of venture capital funds could hinder the development of business plans by potential entrepreneurs. Changes in tax laws, which could dilute an entrepreneur's monetary incentive, generally do not affect an entrepreneur's drive to create his own business. Rather, such factors as independence, creative needs, and desire for control are at the root of an entrepreneur's determination to develop a business. In fact, remuneration is generally the primary motivator in only a small percentage of entrepreneurial activity. In a study to identify the entrepreneurial activity, entrepreneurs indicated their primary motives for starting a new venture as follows:

1. desire for independence (35 percent),
2. desire for increased job satisfaction (25 percent),
3. a release for creative urges (13 percent),
4. financial motivation (13 percent),
5. enjoyment of exploiting business opportunities (11 percent),
6. desire for power/other (3 percent).[1]

Factors such as the perceived availability of venture capital, the pace of technological innovation, and personal motivation have more impact on the development of entrepreneurial talent than the regulatory environment set by government. In the United States, at least, the availability of a pool of entrepreneurial talent that replenishes itself is considered a given.

One final environmental factor which is often taken for granted in the United States is the existence of a large domestic market for a new small business's product. In other countries, notably in Europe, political factors affecting the free flow of products between countries can severely limit the market for an entrepreneurial company's goods. The U.S. GNP, which is as large as the combined GNP of its major European trading partners, provides a large market for new products. Even with the protection and promotion of the European Economic Community, the effective market for goods in Europe is far smaller and more difficult to penetrate than the U.S. market. Additionally, the combination of cultural differences and transportation costs inhibit small European and other nations' firms from marketing their products in the United States.

Venture Capital in Other Countries

With an understanding of the U.S. venture capital experience, it is possible to examine the dimensions of foreign venture capital. Japan, Great Britain, Sweden, France, West Germany, and Israel are trying to develop viable indigenous venture capital industries. While it is tempting to use the strict U.S. definition of venture capital to examine foreign venture capital, this is too narrow a definition to encompass the common forms of foreign venture capital. In the United States, venture capital is the institutionalization of equity investment in emerging companies by the private sector. In foreign countries, this definition must be expanded to include risk capital from any institution, public or private, and this definition should not be limited to institutions specializing only in venture capital.

Japan

Japan is currently in the midst of its second venture capital boom. Its initial boom, which lasted from 1973 to 1975, dissipated following confusion in the

Tokyo stock exchange and the collapse of the Japanese over-the-counter market, both the result of the 1974 oil price shock. Since 1975, venture capital firms which were founded in the initial growth period of 1970 to 1973 have been acting as factoring or commercial finance companies. In 1982 there was a resurgence of venture capital in Japan. In 1983 alone, the Japan Associated Finance Company (JAFCO) raised 23 billion yen (approximately $100 million).[2] This amount represents a significant increase in the capital available for investment, since in 1982 only $84 million of private venture investments were in place.[3]

Motivations behind Japanese venture investments differ from those in the U.S. venture capital industry. Historically, venture capital is practiced in Japan by banks and securities firms, which establish venture capital subsidiaries. The incentive for these firms to enter the venture capital business is to develop future business for their parent firms. Future business can be either in the form of commercial loans or stock offering fees, depending on whether the parent company is a bank or security firm. This industry structure colors the investment analysis of the Japanese venture capitalist since many of the employees of the venture capital firms have come from the parent company and were trained in credit analysis or other short-term investment techniques. The use of short-term analysis is different from the U.S. venture capital concept of nurturing businesses over a five to seven year term. Short-term analysis also leads investment toward later-stage investment, where liquidity will be the highest and capitalization the most secure. It is for this reason that venture investments in Japan are almost always limited to later-stage or bridge financing. Japanese venture capitalists are limited in their investment control since they may not own more than 49 percent of a company's equity.

There is no lack of financial resources for venture capital in Japan. Private investors have adequate incentive to place their funds with venture capitalists since capital gains are not taxed in Japan. Corporations have less of an incentive to invest, however, since capital gains to corporations are taxed at a 50 percent rate. A barrier to venture investment which is larger than the presence or absence of financial incentives is the Japanese attitude toward high-risk investment. Japanese culture places severe penalties on failure and gives practically no reward to exceptional achievement; hence pension fund managers tend to invest only in the most blue of blue-chip stocks. In 1980 Japanese law was changed to enable the free flow of capital between Japan and foreign countries. Since this legislation passed, many Japanese pension funds have invested in U.S. venture capital pools. This step could be an important education for Japanese investors and could portend future investment in domestic pools. In general, financing is not the critical barrier to Japanese venture capital development.

Most Japanese venture capitalists are professionals chosen from the parent company's employee pool. These managers do not have the experience in each phase of a venture company's maturation process. As professionals in the financial industry, they are skilled in credit analysis or stock offering techniques. However, they do not have the experience to aid a portfolio company's development or to assess the worthiness of a business plan that proposes a start-up investment. Hence these venture capitalists lack the skills to implement U.S. venture capital techniques. In addition, the time required to train venture capitalists is a significant barrier to the development of a venture capital industry in Japan. And since earlier Japanese attempts at venture capital failed, there is little domestic experience to draw on.

Perhaps the most serious problem facing the Japanese in their attempt to foster a U.S.-style venture capital industry is the cultural barrier to entrepreneurship and scientific research. In universities, promising young researchers are not given the opportunity to pursue their interests due to the rigid structure of teaching and research positions. Established scientists are culturally bound to their employer through lifetime employment. Even if they had the desire to try their hand at a small business, they receive only the same respect from their peers as if they had continued successfully at their former company. The entrepreneur, in Japan, is a renegade. If he fails, he loses face and has little chance of regaining a job equal to the one he left; if he succeeds, he gains money but little else. For the vast majority of Japanese, financial remuneration remains an inadequate incentive for the perils of entrepreneurship. One factor which may change this norm is the growing number of Western-educated Japanese who are now middle managers, the position many American entrepreneurs held before they left to start their own companies. These persons, because of their experience with the West, may ignore the cultural stigma associated with entrepreneurship.

Recently the Japanese government has taken many steps to encourage the formation of a venture capital industry in Japan. Structurally, the most serious impairment has been the lack of an exit vehicle in the form of either a new issue market or a mergers and acquisitions market. The Osaka Stock Market is Japan's new over-the-counter market and its requirements are very similar to the National Association of Stock Dealers Automated Quotation (NASDAQ) market in the United States. This market may provide venture capitalists with the exit vehicle they have lacked since the mid-1970s. As a backup to the public market, Japanese venture capitalists may soon be able to employ the services of three U.S. investment banking houses which are establishing offices in Tokyo. Citicorp, Salomon Brothers, and Drexel Burnham Lambert are all moving into Japan for the express purpose of participating in the Japanese mergers and acquisitions market.

The Ministry of International Trade and Industry (MITI) is also trying to foster a venture capital climate in Japan through subsidies of research and development. MITI will fund up to half of a company's R&D expenditures when the research is in areas MITI wishes to encourage. And it was MITI that pushed for the formation of the Osaka over-the-counter market. Despite such efforts, however, MITI cannot by legislation or money overcome all the barriers Japan faces in its efforts to establish a U.S.-style venture capital industry. For example, one of the primary means for venture development in the United States is the informal network of lawyers, accountants, bankers, consultants, and successful entrepreneurs who encourage entrepreneurs and recommend them to venture capitalists. Some U.S. firms in Japan are trying to perform this function now. The critical importance of this informal network, however, cannot be overstated.

Great Britain

Venture capital in the United Kingdom, as in Japan, is in a high-growth stage. Of the $300 million to $400 million invested by Europeans worldwide each year, fully half comes from England.[4] British venture capital has had some notable successes with this investment technique, such as Sinclair Computers and Rodime, Inc., but the home market for venture capital is, for the most part, relatively young. Britain's recent development of venture capital is closely correlated with the rise in 1980 of the Unlisted Securities Market, a London Stock Exchange-affiliated over-the-counter market.

Funding for venture capital in the United Kingdom is not sparse. Linked with one of the world's premier financial centers, the venture capital industry in Britain is further complemented with significant portions of foreign venture capital. Indeed, the U.K. venture capital industry is dominated by U.S. venture capital firms. Prominent U.S. venture capital firms, including Alan Patricoff Associates, Citicorp, and TA Associates, have all established London-based firms in the past two years. These firms are more than foreign offices of their U.S. affiliates; between them, they control approximately $55 million for investment. British law also gives investors promise of good liquidity for venture firms that go public. Since 1979, Britain has allowed a $7,500 annual write-off against personal income taxes for investments in unlisted public companies.[5]

Britain has a distinct advantage over other countries in trying to expand a U.S.-style venture capital industry. As an English speaking country, Britain can readily import U.S. trained venture capitalists or send employees to the United States for training. In culture and style of business, the United States and the United Kingdom are sufficiently similar to exchange professionals, a fact which can speed the development of the country's venture capital industry.

Although British entrepreneurs possess the entrepreneurial initiative, they are not yet as experienced as are their U.S. counterparts in venture capital.[6] The government has recently given them a boost by announcing that its research and development funding arm, the British Technology Group, will no longer automatically have exclusive patent rights to any project it funds, but will share them with the private sector.

Sweden

Venture capital in Sweden is expanding at a rate similar to the British venture capital industry. There are about thirty venture capital companies now operating in Sweden, and most of them have been established within the past two years. The largest pool of venture capital in Sweden, the Four Seasons Venture Capital AB, was established in early 1983 with a total capitalization of $13.5 million. Investors in the pool include two Swedish pension funds, private Swedish investors, and U.S. interests.[7]

The primary reason Sweden has not developed a venture capital industry prior to the current boom has been the disincentives for investment in equity funds of any type. Due to double taxation, investors before 1982 could only receive 6.75 percent of pretax corporate earnings. From that money, Swedes would have to pay a wealth tax of 1.5 to 3.0 percent of the book value of their shares. (Corporate taxes in Sweden are 58 percent and personal income taxes are as high as 85 percent.) It is not uncommon to find taxpayers whose taxes exceed their income. These tax rates compare unfavorably with other countries in Europe. In West Germany, for example, investors receive 44 percent of pretax corporate income, and even in the Netherlands, a country well known for its high taxes and welfare state, investors receive 14.6 percent of pretax corporate income. The United States compares favorably with a maximum rate of return of 27 percent, and in Great Britain investors receive 25 percent.[8]

Recognizing the implications of this disincentive, Sweden has recently changed the tax laws to stimulate investment in small companies. Family-owned and over-the-counter firms may now deduct up to 70 percent of their dividends from taxation, thereby increasing net receipts from corporate profits to approximately 20 percent. In addition, Sweden now taxes wealth at 30 percent of book value for small and medium-sized firms. The net effect of this legislation is to make small and medium-sized companies a tax shelter rather than a tax burden.[9]

Swedish venture capitalists are still inexperienced, but there are some factors that will help the development of a Swedish venture capital industry. First, the over-the-counter market was instituted in 1983. Second, small companies in Sweden have strong ties with banks because of traditionally high debt-to-equity ratios. This may enable banks to become facilitators or conduits between venture capitalists and entrepreneurs.

Sweden's high level of entrepreneurship is its greatest attraction to venture capitalists. Not counting farms or inactive companies, there are 200,000 firms in Sweden, or one for every forty-two Swedes. This translates into one entrepreneur for every ten Swedes working in non-agricultural jobs.[10] With its highly educated population, Sweden could become very attractive to venture capitalists.

France

Because of conflicting signs from the socialist government under Francois Mitterand, the future of French venture capital is the most difficult of all European countries to assess. On the one hand, capital gains taxes have been reduced to 15 percent, and a new over-the-counter market has been developed to trade the issues of small and medium-sized companies. On the other hand, personal income taxes have been raised to 65 percent, with an additional 10 percent surcharge on taxes paid; a wealth tax of between 0.5 and 1.5 percent has been instituted, and the rules for a new listing on the over-the-counter market require that so little of a firm's stock be publicly held that almost no liquidity for many stocks exists. Analysts fear that while the wealth tax could force many privately held companies onto the market in order to pay the owner's wealth tax, there may be no market for these securities as wealthy persons attempt to keep their wealth invisible from the government's taxes.[11]

Considering the advantageous capital gains tax rate, the basic incentives for a successful venture capital industry in France appear to be present. French venture capitalists also have some experience in U.S.-style venture capital investments. Paribus, one of France's leading banks, has had venture capital funds in the United States and Japan since 1981 with a total pool of capital of $35 and $20 million respectively.[12] This direct venture capital experience could be a valuable impetus to the development of French venture capital. Whether sufficient entrepreneurial activity exists in France to achieve a vibrant venture capital industry remains to be seen. Paribus, however, sees its foreign capital funds as providing a window on technology in the more advanced countries. This window could help stimulate creativity and entrepreneurship in France through technology transfer.

West Germany

Neither the private sector nor the government appears to have yet embraced the concept of venture capital for West Germany. What venture capital does exist is either noninstitutionalized or foreign. Two factors account for the lack of venture capital in West Germany: the absence of an over-the-counter market and the risk-averse nature of both investors and potential entrepreneurs.

Potential investors for a venture capital industry are present in West Germany, a fact demonstrated by the approximately $100 million that Germans have invested in U.S. venture capital partnerships. The majority of this money, however, comes from private investors rather than institutional investors.[13] These private investors have invested in venture capital because of the consistent and profitable rates of return demonstrated over 30 years. While these funds were raised by Germans, few Germans have yet to gain experience in the actual investment of the money. German investors could provide a formidable pool of venture capital because of their high rate of savings, which annually exceeds 15 percent of income. Tax laws now favor equity investment since in the last five years the double taxation of corporate profits has been substantially reduced. Nevertheless, German investors tend to favor fixed-income securities over equity issues.

While there are a few West German venture capital firms, they are small, new, and foreign controlled. Without an over-the-counter market to give venture capital investments liquidity, venture capital as an industry cannot hope to develop. There are other problems as well. In the past ten years fewer than twenty new stock issues have been floated in West Germany, with half of them occurring in the past year. West German bankers who have the monopoly on stockbrokerage activities are inexperienced in floating new issues. Besides, they would rather lend these companies money than have them raise equity in the public market. The tradition of debt financing in Germany is strong. For example, in 1965 the average equity as a percentage of total assets stood at 29.5 percent; by 1981 that figure had reached 20.5 percent. Venture capital in West Germany, therefore, must overcome a variety of structural barriers if it is to develop.[14]

Israel

Venture capital as a distinct industry does not exist in Israel. Israel does boast a fair amount of venture capital, however, and the Israeli government has implicitly acknowledged the desirability of venture capital investment in Israel. Recognizing that the country is burdened with a huge international debt, has few natural resources other than its people, and must support a tremendous military expense, it has targeted high technology as its best hope to improve its economic situation. Israel recognizes the potentially beneficial role venture capital can play in the development of high-technology industries.

To stimulate venture capital investment in Israel, the Israeli government has begun to subsidize research and development in small firms. In 1977 Israel created an Office of Chief Scientists within the Ministry of Industry and Trade. This office can match dollar for dollar a company's investments in projects which it deems promising. Further funding may be obtained from the Israel–United States Binational Industrial Research and Development

Foundation, commonly known as Bird F. This foundation provides loans for developing ideas involving businesses in both the United States and Israel. Bird F is funded with $60 million, half of which comes from the U.S. government and the other half from the Israeli government.[15]

Private firms have also begun targeting venture capital for investment opportunities. At least two major banks, the Israel Discount Bank and Bank Leumi, have venture capital subsidiaries, and Bank Hapoalim, which is owned by Israel's largest labor union, is participating by raising venture capital through the issuance of debt instruments abroad. In order to gain the liquidity necessary to liquidate venture investments, Israeli entrepreneurs have tapped both the Israeli and U.S. equity markets. Indeed, at least a dozen Israeli companies are traded on either the NASDAQ or American Stock Exchange.

Summary

Clearly, the concept of venture capital, with its dynamic impact on a nation's economy, has intrigued both the public and private sectors of many foreign countries. While it is evident that the U.S. experience in venture capital has influenced these countries greatly, it is also clear that a venture capital industry is shaped by the customs and culture of the country where it is practiced. Even if the attempts to adapt venture capital to other countries are only half as beneficial to those countries as venture capital has been to the United States, the attempts will be considered highly successful.

Notes

1. "The Role of Venture Capital in the EEC," *European Trends*, January, 1983.

2. "Venture Capital In Japan: Scramble for Firms to Invest In," *Oriental Economist*, November 1983, p. 10.

3. "Japan: Smoothing the Way for Venture Capital—Again," *Business Week*, October 11, 1982, p. 53.

4. "Entrepreneurs Come of Age on the Continent," *Business Week*, December 12, 1983, p. 45.

5. Ibid.

6. Dave Lindoff, "The U.K.'s Three New Venture Funds," *Venture*, April 1982, p. 50.

7. "Doors Open for Venture Capital," *Sweden Now*, November 1983, p. 20.

8. "A Touch of Capitalism," *Forbes*, May 9, 1983, p. 120.

9. "Doors Open for Venture Capital."

10. "A Touch of Capitalism."

11. Ibid.

12. "The Big Money Paribas is Betting on Overseas Ventures," *Business Week*, December 12, 1983, p. 45.

13. *American Banker*, June 24, 1984, p. 13.

14. "West German Venture Capital," *New York Times*, June 6, 1983, p. D7.

15. Jean A. Briggs, "We Need Entrepreneurs, Not Military Heroes," *Forbes*, November 7, 1984, p. 140.

6
Technology Venturing

The scientific, technological, and economic preeminence of the United States depends on the strength, vigor, and dynamism of our unique entrepreneurial American culture. Capital venturing is a critical component of this culture. The United States has maintained, and will continue to maintain, its preeminence because of our abilities to encourage the emergence of the high-technology venture business; expand our venture capital markets; restructure and reform our financial and security markets; and collaborate, as required, on R&D systems between our public- and private-sector institutions. America's strength has always been our ability to be scientifically creative, technologically adept, managerially innovative, and entrepreneurially daring. In these ways, we have met and will continue to meet critical challenges in order to promote the common good and provide for the general welfare.

This book has had two broad purposes. First, it has sought to provide a framework or context for understanding the venture capital process. Second, it has been intended to provide a perspective on the future of participative creativity. Participative creativity concerns our involvement—personally, professionally and institutionally—in the transformation that is taking place in the United States and the world.

To accomplish these two purposes, this book has focused on a set of themes that are having an impact on our values, our private enterprise system, and the very nature of our society. These themes incorporate and reflect how we finance, manage, and control our institutions; what data, information, and knowledge are required to utilize advances in technology; and how the emerging interrelationships among academia, government, and business are affecting society.

Drivers for Society

Science and technology are societal drivers. Drivers are those catalysts that change the composition of society, including its institutions. They have dramatic impacts on the nation, individual states, and local communities. They affect the viability of our industries, the growth and survivability of our

business enterprises, and the role, scope, and purpose of emerging private/
public sector institutions.

Science and technology are altering American society. Today's environment for change is fundamentally different from that of even a decade ago.
The process of change has been dramatically accelerated. The "old
economy" emphasized cheap and abundant natural resources, borrowing
over savings, growth over efficiency, and quantity over quality. The "new
economy," however, is reversing these trends.

Solutions to critical issues and problems now demand an integrated,
holistic, flexible approach that blends technological, managerial, scientific,
financial, cultural, and political ramifications in an atmosphere of extreme
time compression.

Integrating the eclectic branches of science, converting them into technological resources, and then creating business opportunities are all part of the
capital venturing process. Indeed, in an environment of increasing time compression and in a period characterized by a scientific/technological/knowl-
edge integration explosion, it is well to recall the remarks of the philosopher
Alfred North Whitehead:

> . . . the role of progress is such that individual human beings of ordinary
> length of life will be called upon to face novel situations which find no
> parallel in their past. The fixed person, who for the fixed duties in older
> societies was such a god-send, in the future will be a public danger.[1]

Lewis M. Branscomb, vice president and chief scientist of IBM, has identified
a critical emerging issue for the "new economy":

> Indeed—since computer applications are designed to serve human needs—
> one must frequently depend more on humanistic experience and common
> sense than on science to determine how a computer system should be ar-
> ranged.[2]

The principles enunciated by Whitehead and Branscomb have far-reach-
ing impacts, and relate directly to the importance of a vibrant venture capital
industry. The demands that the last two decades of the 20th century will im-
pose on our society and our institutions involve the increasing development
of people for nonparallel, novel tasks. We are seeing the rise of emerging
technological industries, which are concerned with nonroutine kinds of problems that require a new order of solution. These emerging and expanding
industries include space commerce; macroengineering; control of environmental, water, and air pollution; transportation; health care; waste management; biotechnology; computers and communications; and robotics. At the
same time, we are seeing that science and technology are the resources that re-
vitalize our basic industries and services.

The venture capital industry in the United States will help to shape a number of key issues for policy makers at all levels in both the public and private sectors:

1. What will be the 21st century industries in the United States? How will their development be financed? What will be their markets?
2. How will society create and allocate wealth and income?
3. How will new forms of organizations change institutions to fit societal as well as individual needs in a stable, sustainable society?

There are three underlying requirements to these issues. First, they demand large quantities of technical and intellectual resources such as individual scientists (social and physical), engineers, and other professionals, as well as service personnel and technicians as aides to the professionals. Second, they require relevant and up-to-date knowledge necessary for the solution of nonroutine problems. Third, they need people with the abilities to identify and formulate the problems for solution. In other words, we need a new breed of creative and innovative entrepreneurs and *intra*preneurs (managers in larger firms who possess entrepreneurial abilities) who can operate in the changing risk-taking and risk-sharing environment required by technology venturing.

In the old economy, management decision making centered on efficiency and effectiveness. In the new economy, management decision making must rely on flexibility and adaptability to deal with rapid and external technological changes. This is what the venture capitalist brings to new enterprises.

Externally, the forces for transformation are our educational system and the burgeoning bureaucratic infrastructure of governmental policies and regulations. Managers of all our institutions are facing pressures resulting from changes in demographics and in public attitudes, concerns, and lifestyles. They must deal with demands imposed by the utilization of economic wealth and national resources, political philosophies, international trade barriers, and the rapid escalation of new clusters of technologies for the 1980s and 1990s.

The consequences from this myriad of interlinking forces are real and extend to more than economic growth or stagnation. Indeed, the consequences may well determine the future form of our society, the shifting socioeconomic make-up of our regions, the changing loci of leadership, and emerging inter-institutional functional networks.

The simpler distinctions between owner and entrepreneur or between professional manager and venture manager have to a large extent disappeared in the past decade. Private managerial functions have been altered and extended by newer and more complex organizational structures, financial arrangements, governmental regulations and relations, changes in generally accepted ethics and morals, and advances in technology. In other words, our society and its economic infrastructure have changed dramatically, resulting in a wide gap between the management knowledge base and the practice of management. The venture capitalist can help deal with these changes by bringing a variety of resources to new enterprises.

The personnel requirements for the emerging technologies are creating a major societal displacement. Millions of workers in the manufacturing, service, and administrative sectors who have done only repetitive jobs now need to acquire new skills. Technological change is having three dramatic impacts on the general work force, not just passive acceptance of new ways but active collaboration. In this context, participative creativity means (1) increased flexibility in the workplace, (2) the advent of new institutional arrangements, and (3) the customization of products and services.

Technology Venturing

The new economy is emerging in our society as the result of intense global competition, both scientific and economic. International scientific competition is concentrated on the efforts of each nation and its respective institutions to become preeminent in a selected or targeted area. No better example exists than the "supercomputer." The Japanese objectives for the fifth generation computer have triggered governmental responses in England and the European community as well as the formation of research and development consortiums of private companies in the United States and Europe. Venture capital will play a prominent role in the subsequent economic competition for next generation computers. There are already signs that our academic institutions and advanced government and business research laboratories are preparing many scientific and advanced engineering programs and projects woven around the supercomputer.

As a result of increasing international competition, we are witnessing the development of an emerging American phenomenon—technology venturing. Technology venturing is the process by which major institutions take and share risk in integrating and commercializing scientific research and various technologies. It is a primary means of generating innovative products and services of economic value, particularly through a vibrant venture capital industry. To compete effectively in the global economic arena, we need to find creative and innovative ways to link public-sector initiatives and private-sector investments. What entrepreneurship does for small business, technology venturing can do for corporations, universities, consortiums, and governments. Thus technology venturing is a catalyst for a broad-based emergent entrepreneurial spirit in America.

To better understand technology venturing, it is necessary to review briefly the commercialization process. Commercialization is the process by which the results of research and development are introduced into products and services in the marketplace. In other words, commercialization requires a closer integration of economics with science and technology. Its implementation demands new collaborative ties between government, academia, and business. Commercialization requires the interchange of ideas and opinions that are technological in nature, for example, choices between technology making and technology taking. The taking is in terms of venture capital formation, entrepreneurship, interfirm cooperation, establishment of university-based development centers, evaluating new technology, and monitoring technological trends. Commercialization also helps to define the educational and training requirements for present and emerging marketplaces. Commercialization can thus be a major driving force that invigorates new businesses and rejuvenates basic industries.

Technology, like innovation, is a much overused word. It is therefore appropriate to ask, "How does technology originate?" What is clear is that institutions are performing basic research, applied research, and developmental research that result in scientific knowledge and technical know-how as well as products and services that are ready to be marketed. These are commercialized through various means including product development, *intra*preneurship, entrepreneurship, new business incubators, robust growth companies, and capital venturing.

In other words, the ability to take scientific knowledge and technical know-how, and convert them into profitable technology resources, as shown in figure 6-1 is part of the capital venturing process. Any breakthrough can well provide practical decision-making know-how for managers and entrepreneurs, and productive investments and opportunities for business firms. Transforming science into a technological resource, however, has traditionally been predominantly entrusted to scientists and advanced engineers. Today venture capitalists are becoming more directly involved.

Figure 6-2 on the commercialization process illustrates that there are a set of institutions that are sources for R&D: for example, government, industry, and nonprofit institutions. There are others which are the performers of R&D: for example, government laboratories, industry, universities and colleges, and other nonprofit institutions.

Although scientific knowledge is reposited in schools, libraries, and a variety of other public and private institutions, the commercialization of science to a technological resource is not yet a well-defined academic field. The transfer of technical knowledge to technological resources is a better understood process. Technical knowledge, for example, is transformed into patents or know-how and then subsequent licensing and cross-licensing

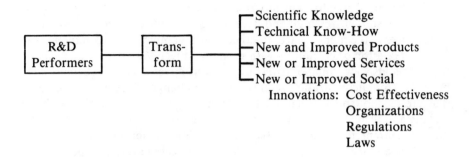

Figure 6–1. Transforming Science

agreements. In this context, multinational corporations have produced a wholesale transfer of scientific and technological knowledge across national frontiers. The efficiency and effectiveness as well as the flexibility and adaptability of the commercialization of scientific and technological knowledge into practically useful resources are fresh areas for academic research.

Basic research—scientific knowledge and breakthroughs—is perhaps less subject to security restrictions and is still predominantly thought of in Jeffersonian terms as a "free world good." Even with the relatively free access of all institutions and nations to scientific breakthroughs, the actual implementation or commercialization of the emerging technologies is dependent upon the degree of stagnation in the old technologies, the attractiveness of the new alternatives, and the ability to finance and manage new ventures.

Frank Davidson, an international lawyer and chairman of the System Dynamics Steering Committee at the Alfred P. Sloan School of Management at MIT, points to the importance of new kinds of relationships in which science and technology will shape our future:

> Modern science, meanwhile, has added the armory of advanced technology— the new capabilities of computer science, telecommunications, ballistics, and so on—to humankind's ancient ability to organize masses of people for large-scale work; if we are to benefit from the consequent increase in the scale, range, and impact of "Big Technology," there will have to be a transformation in our behavior, our institutions, and—not least—in our vocabulary. We shall have to abandon the sterile political rhetoric of "public sector" versus "private sector," and learn instead the neglected arts of intersectoral harmony and collaboration.[3]

The need for intersectoral harmony and collaboration arises from the nature and type of international competition that confronts the United States;

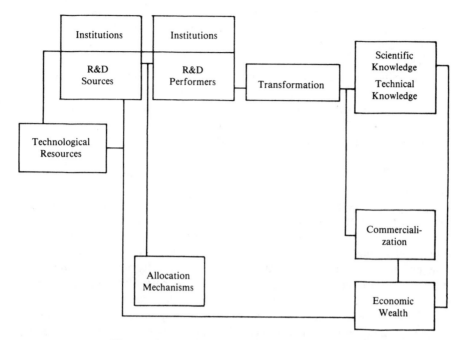

Figure 6-2. The Commercialization Process

the rules of the game have changed. As a result, there is a dramatic change in the R&D environment. The federal government, state governments, universities and colleges, and other nonprofit institutions are committing substantial R&D investments that will be a major stimulant to our economy. The resultant newer technologies and their spin-offs create the need to make choices for commercialization across a broad front. In fact, they force us to select while still in the R&D phase those products and services in which we may excel either scientifically or economically.

America's future depends on our abilities to support and then diffuse, through innovation, the newer technologies of the 1980s. Through their use, we can strengthen our nation's defense posture while improving our domestic and international economic positions. The emerging technologies can become our nation's growth industries that will help to stimulate a robust economy in the decades ahead.

The introduction of the fourth industrial revolution cluster of innovations into the marketplace is a complex phenomenon. It is not simply a case of adapting a technology to production of a product or service. The sciences and technologies are so numerous and interrelated that integration is a key element. The better one can integrate these in a commercialization process, the more effective the chain reaction and the stronger the competitive market position. This is why a strong and diversified venture capital industry can be so important to economic development.

The U.S. strategy has been to institutionalize the bulk of basic research in universities, colleges, and nonprofit institutions. Most applied research and development has been institutionalized in industry. Commercialization to meet new market demands has been left to individual institutions. As a result, a critical dimension for issue identification and policy making in the future is simply keeping up with the myriad of advances and potential breakthroughs in science and technology regardless of the source of funds for research. This is far more than what has been referred to as the "information explosion."

Little managerial research and development has been directed towards handling this "integration explosion" in the United States until recently. Fortunately, there are now some beginnings in the private sector and in the public sector on the state level to tackle this problem. Newer institutional arrangements must become a high priority if we are to meet and overcome future international competition, such as the Japanese fifth generation computer which threatens to supersede U.S. computer preeminance.

To meet these challenges, research and development and its subsequent commercialization must take place within newer institutional arrangements, such as consortiums and incubators. More cooperation and collaborative involvement is necessary among those institutions that perform basic research, those that do applied and developmental research, those that are the sources of R&D funding, and those that do subsequent commercialization. Emerging cooperative networks can do more than better disseminate the exploding body of knowledge. They can help resolve problems that arise from financing and managing new enterprises. These institutional arrangements, by permitting more flexibility and adaptability in assessing and implementing research and technology, can assist in meeting the nation's needs for economic diversification, job creation, and entrepreneurial talent.

A short time ago, managers of most of our companies saw collaboration as a high-risk alternative. They tended to be secretive about their firms' operations, played their cards extremely close to their chests, and often considered joint R&D ventures as low priority opportunities. But the United States is in a new era of international scientific and economic competition. Consequently, institutions in the public, private, and nonprofit sectors are recognizing new entrepreneurial styles and organizations for maintaining the overall competitive position of our industries internationally while providing the means for individual firm creativity.

The United States can win a scientific race but that does not ensure economic success in a global market. Other nations have become adept at applying U.S. scientific advances to their own needs while improving their manufacturing, financial, marketing, and managerial abilities to compete vigorously in international markets. Japan, the United Kingdom, and perhaps the European community will in the future focus more strongly on research and development and the innovation process, and may be as effective in the scientific competition as the United States. As a result, each nation may gain in prestige from its own unique scientific research, organizational R&D structures, and massing of technological and human resources.

In this context, the ability to market a product a few months or a few years earlier may be of great value to an individual firm's well-being and that of its immediate community. Current economic theory does not emphasize this critical time component; economic theory has not advanced to the point where it can cope with the rapid diffusion of scientific advances, extremely short technological life cycles, ever-increasing fixed-capital investments with shorter economic lives than allowed by IRS regulations or tax incentives, comparatively brief generation times for new products, and the rapid appearance and disappearance of markets. In summary, economic theory itself needs to be subjected to intense study to handle these newer classes of problems—and more specifically to measure firms' and nations' efficiency, effectiveness, flexibility, and adaptability in a global market economy when competing with many sophisticated and highly industrialized nations.

Technology venturing is an integrative process. It incorporates a dynamic venture capital industry; a creative role for government through federal, state, and local technology policies, initiatives, and development programs; and newer academic relationships. It also fosters corporate and community collaborative efforts while nurturing positive government/academic/business relationships.

Technology venturing is essential in improving our educational structure, fulfilling critical manpower requirements, and enhancing our industrial creativity and innovation. It is a primary means for encouraging the emergence of a myriad of technology-venture businesses in the context of a private-enterprise system that has always been the unique American way to achieve and maintain U.S. economic, scientific, and technological preeminence.

Notes

1. Alfred North Whitehead, *Science and the Modern World,* (New York: The Free Press, 1925), p. 196.

2. Lewis M. Branscomb, "The Computer's Debt to Science," *Perspectives in Computing,* vol. 3, no. 3, October 1983, p. 4.

3. Frank Davidson, *Macro: A Clear Vision of How Science and Technology Will Shape Our Future,* (New York: William Morrow and Company, Inc., 1983), p. 16.

Appendixes

Appendix A:
The Texas Venture Capital Industry

Compared to the nation's venture capital centers in New York, San Francisco, and Boston, the Texas venture capital industry is embryonic. Currently, there are at least seventy-three venture capital organizations based in Texas which include sixteen private partnerships, one business development company and fifty-six Small Business Investment Companies. In addition, at least seven venture capital partnerships have established offices in Texas. Texas venture capital organizations have $528 million of capitalized funds available for venture investment and Texas SBICs have an additional $113 million of small business administration leverage.[1] Since the nationwide pool of venture capital in 1983 totaled $11.5 billion, Texas' share of the industry is only 4.5 percent.[2] While the nation's venture capital pool has increased 72 percent over its 1982 total of $6.7 billion, in the same period Texas' venture capital pool has increased by 100 percent over its 1982 pool of $259 million.

The state's sixteen venture capital partnerships and one business development company control $363.2 million of venture capital, or 70 percent of the state's total. Texas' fifty-six small business investment companies (SBICs) control the remaining $158 million. These totals, however, do not include reinvested profits, SBA leverage for SBICs, or contributed funds in excess of capitalization, so the figure for available funds is somewhat conservative. But this gap is inherent in all venture capital industry statistics, so Texas' current position in the national venture capital picture is not altered. Table A-1 presents selected partnerships and SBICs with their capitalizations arranged by geographic location.

As table A-1 illustrates, Dallas has emerged as the primary venture capital center in Texas, with a $286 million venture capital pool. Of this total, $205 million is controlled by eight venture capital partnerships. In Houston, SBICs control $64 million of venture money but, with two exceptions, these SBICs are small by venture capital standards. Venture capital partnerships in Houston are also small and control only $7.5 million. San Antonio has $86 million of venture capital, $74.5 million of which is managed by Southwest Venture Partners, the oldest venture capital firm in the state. Austin has $82 million of venture capital, $66 million of which was raised by three venture capital partnerships in 1984. There is an additional $62 million controlled by ten other SBICs across the state.

During the last two years, the growth of the Texas venture capital has been the result of venture capital partnerships. 1983 saw the establishment of nine venture capital partnerships. Sevin, Rosen, Bayless, Borovoy raised $60 million for its Dallas-based partnership which, in 1981, had capitalized a $25 million partnership called Sevin Rosen Ventures. Barry Cash Venture Partners raised $25 million in 1983, as did Southwest Enterprise Associates, both based in Dallas. Lexington Venture Partners and Texas Venture Partners, which are associated organizations, raised $15 million over the 1983–1984 period in Dallas. In San Antonio the outgrowth of the old Hixon Venture Capital Firm, Southwest Venture Partners, closed a $42.5 million fund in October 1983. In Austin three significant venture capital funds were capitalized in 1984: Triad Ventures, an outgrowth of FSA Capital, raised $30 million; Rust Ventures L.P., an outgrowth of the Rust Capital SBIC, raised $28 million, and Business Development Partners capitalized a $7.8 million follow-on fund. Houston also added its first three venture capital partnerships, capitalized at a total of $7.5 million.

The fact that these funds are located in Texas does not mean that all their investments are made in the state. Over the 1980 to 1983 period, Texas venture capital organizations placed only 36 percent of their investment dollars in-state, with the remainder spread around the nation.[3] The percentage of investments in Texas by Texas-based venture capitalists is illustrated in figure A–1. Of 61 selected Texas investments by Texas-based venture capitalists, 38 percent went to oil and gas related businesses, while 30 percent went to fund high-technology endeavors, including communications, biotechnology, semiconductor, and computer-related firms. Table A–2 on venture capital disbursements demonstrates the distribution of venture capital investments in Texas by technology area. This table highlights two significant aspects of Texas venture capital. First, investments are weighted toward oil- and gas-related businesses. Most of these companies, however, were funded prior to the industry's 1982 cyclical downturn. Second, high technology is receiving a disproportionately low percentage of Texas-based venture capital financing. Whereas high technology received over 70 percent of venture capitalists' commitments nationwide, Texas-based venture firms disbursed only 30 percent of their funds to high-technology firms.[4]

Texas venture capitalists, however, are not unique in focusing on what appear to be dual trends toward energy investments and away from high technology. Investments in Texas firms by venture capitalists nationwide followed similar patterns. From 1980 to 1983, 54 percent of disbursements by all venture capitalists to Texas firms were to energy-related companies. Texas firms whose products fall into either the computer-related communications,

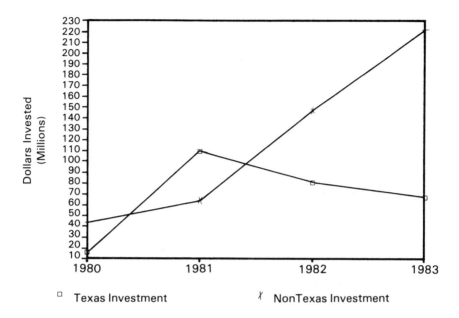

Source: David T. Thompson, "Venture Capital and Financing," unpublished speech, "Technology Venturing: American Innovation and Risk-Taking," conference, February 7, 1984, Dallas, Texas.

Figure A-1. Texas-Based Venture Capital Investment: Geographic Distribution, 1980 to 1983

other electronics, or biotechnology categories received only 31 percent of disbursements[5] (see table A-3). The IC[2] database shows that among 21 giant venture capital firms' investments in Texas, 67 percent of the companies backed were energy-related and 75 percent of the money invested went to these firms. While the sample of the giant venture capital firms' investments is not sufficiently large to be conclusive, it has proved to be a valuable leading indicator of venture capital investments in the past. This sample would confirm the possible trend toward investments in a mature and cyclical industry and away from high-technology emerging industries.

Table A-4 shows investments of individual venture capital firms by technology. Table A-5 shows investments of individual venture capital firms by state.

An additional source of funds to broaden these investment trends may be out-of-state venture capital firms that are being attracted to Texas. For example, in 1983 and 1984, seven partnerships have opened offices in Dallas: Citicorp Venture Capital of New York; Investments Orange Nassau of Boston and the Netherlands; Golder Thoma and Company, and Woodland Capital of Chicago; Intercapco of Cleveland; Business Resource Investors, and Dougery, Jones & Wilder, both of California. Table A–6 provides a directory of investments by selected venture institutions.

Notes

1. IC^2 database, The University of Texas at Austin.
2. *Venture Capital Journal,* November 1983, p. 6.
3. David T. Thompson, "Venture Capital and Financing," Unpublished speech, "Technology Venturing: American Innovation and Risk-Taking," conference, February 7, 1984, Dallas, Texas.
4. "Venture Capitalists Invest $2.8 Billion in 1983," *Venture Capital Journal,* May 1984, p. 8.
5. Thompson, "Venture Capital and Financing."

Table A-1
Summary of Texas Venture Capital Institutions
(millions of dollars)

	Capitalization	Leverage (SBICs Only)
Austin		
Venture Capital Partnerships		
Rubicon Group	5.0	
Triad Ventures	30.0	
Rust Ventures, L.P.	28.0	
Business Development Partners	10.4	
SBICs		
FSA Capital	2.0	0
Rust Capital	7.0	6.0
Sub-total—Austin	82.4	6.0
Dallas		
Venture Capital Partnerships		
Barry Cash	25.0	
Capital Southwest	39.6	
Innovative Growth Ventures	6.0	
Lexington/Texas Venture Partners	15.0	
MSI Capital	na	
Sevin, Rosen, Bayless, Borovoy	85.0	
Southwest Enterprise Associates	25.0	
Sunwestern Investment	9.0	
SBICs		
BancTexas Capital	1.0	0
Brittany Capital	0.5	1.6
Business Capital Corp.	0.5	0.5
Capital Marketing Corp.	8.9	26.4
Commerce Southwest Capital	1.0	na
CSC Capital Corp.	4.1	6.0
Dallas Business Capital	6.3	na
Diman Financial Corp.	0.5	na
Equity Capital	0.5	0
First Dallas Central Corp.	16.0	na
Interfirst Capital	12.5	7.2
Mercantile Dallas	11.5	28.0
MESBIC of Dallas	2.0	na
Republic Venture Group	12.0	0
Richardson Capital Corp.	1.0	0
Sunwestern SBIC	2.0	0
Trammell Crow	0.5	0
West Texas Central Capital	1.0	na
National Venture Capital Firms with Dallas Offices		
Business Resource Investors—California		
Citicorp Venture Capital—New York		
Dougery, Jones & Wilder—San Francisco		
Golder Thoma—Chicago		
Intercapco—Cleveland		
Investments Orange Nassau—Boston, The Netherlands		
Woodland Capital—Chicago		
Sub-total—Dallas	286.4	70.0

	Capitalization	Leverage (SBICs Only)
Houston		
Venture Capital Partnerships		
Criterion	na	
Houston Venture Investors	5.0	
MND Venture Capital Corp.	2.5	
Rotan Mosle Technology Partners/Taylor & Turner	na	
SBICs		
Allied Bancshares Capital	13.0	0
American Energy Investments	2.5	2.5
Americap Corp.	1.0	0
Aspen Financial	0.5	na
Bow Lane Capital	2.5	7.5
Charter Venture Group	1.0	0
Energy Assets, Inc.	0.6	0.5
Energy Capital	11.3	0
Enterprise Capital	2.5	2.5
Evergreen Capital	2.0	na
First Business Investment	0.5	na
First City Capital	0.5	1.6
Grocers SBI Corp.	0.5	1.0
Livingston Capital	1.0	1.9
Mapleleaf Capital	3.3	2.0
Rainbow Capital	0.5	na
Red River Ventures	0.8	1.8
Retail Capital	0.5	1.5
Retzloff Capital Corp.	2.5	0
Rice Investment Co.	1.8	3.7
SBI Capital	1.8	0.5
Texas Capital	3.0	7.9
Texas Commerce	5.1	0
Zenith Capital	0.5	na
Sub-total—Houston	66.6	35.0
San Antonio		
Venture Capital Partnerships		
Southwest Venture Partners	74.5	
SBICs		
Gill Capital Corporation	10.0	0
San Antonio Venture Group	1.0	0
Cameron Financial	0.5	na
Sub-total—San Antonio	86.0	0
Other		
SBICs		
Central Texas SBI—Waco	0.3	0.1
First Bancorp Capital—Corsicana	0.5	na
First Capital Corp.—Fort Worth	1.0	na
Great American Capital—Wichita Falls	0.5	na
Omega Capital Corp.—Beaumont	0.5	0
Permian Basin Capital—Midland	0.5	na
Rice Country Capital—Eagle Lake	0.4	0
South Texas SBIC—Victoria	1.0	1.0
Southwestern Venture Corp.—Seguin	1.0	0
TSM Corp.—El Paso	0.5	1.2
Sub-total—other	6.2	2.3
Total	527.6	113.3

Table A-2
Venture Capital Disbursements in Texas by Technology
(Percent)

Technology	Distribution
Oil and gas related	38
Communications	16
Computer related	8
Health Services	7
Manufacturing	7
Retail	5
Semiconductors	3
Medical Technology	3
Other (e.g., printing, automotive)	13

Table A-3
Venture Capital Investments in Texas, 1980 to 1983
(millions of dollars)

	1980	1981	1982	1983	Total 1980 to 1983
Communications	14.3	36.2	29.1	7.5	87.1
Computer-Related	2.0	6.5	28.8	45.8	83.1
Other Electronics	0.4	1.6	2.2	0.0	4.2
Biotechnology	0.0	0.5	0.0	0.0	0.5
Medical-Related	0.0	0.0	17.9	12.0	29.9
Energy-Related	108.8	89.7	56.6	41.9	297.0
Consumer-Related	1.1	0.0	2.0	4.5	7.6
Industrial Products	3.8	2.4	2.0	1.6	9.8
Other	2.0	28.6	3.0	0.4	34.0
Total	132.4	165.5	141.6	113.7	553.2

Source: Thompson, David T., "Venture Capital and Financing." Unpublished speech, "Technology Venturing: American Innovation and Risk-Taking," conference, February 7, 1984, Dallas, Texas.

Table A-4
Selected Venture Investment Institutions: Investment by Technology

	Computer Related	Robotics	Medical	Tele-communications	Manu-facturing	Oil and Gas Related	Semi-Conductor	Broad-casting	Food Service	Other
Dallas										
Venture Capital Partnerships										
Capital Southwest $39.6 million	X	—	X	X	X	X	—	X	—	X
Barry Cash $25.0 million	X	—	—	X	—	—	—	—	—	—
MSI Capital Capitalization Unavailable	—	—	—	X	X	—	—	—	—	X
Southwest Enterprise Associates $25.0 million	X	—	—	X	—	—	X	—	—	—
Sunwestern Investment $9.0 million	X	—	X	X	X	X	X	—	—	—
Sevin Rosen Partners $85.0 million	X	—	X	X	—	—	X	—	—	X
Texas Venture Partners $15.0 million	X	—	—	X	—	—	X	—	—	—
SBICs										
Brittany Capital $0.5 million	—	—	—	—	X	X	—	X	X	—
Commerce Southwest Capital $1.0 million	—	—	—	—	—	X	—	—	—	—
Interfirst Venture[a] $12.5 million	X	—	X	X	X	X	X	X	X	X
MESBIC of Dallas $2.0 million	X	—	—	—	—	X	—	—	X	—
Republic Venture Group[a] $12.0 million	X	—	X	X	X	X	—	—	—	—
Total Capitalization $266.9 million										

Houston

Venture Capital Partnerships

Rotan Mosie Technology Partners
$ 3.2 million

SBICs

Allied Bancshares Capital[a]
$11.7 million

American Energy Investment
$ 2.5 million

Bow Lane Capital
$ 2.5 million

Charter Venture Group[a]
$ 2.0 million

Energy Capital
$12.0 million

Evergreen Capital
$ 2.0 million

Red River Ventures
Capitalization Unknown

SBI Capital
$ 1.0 million

Texas Capital[a]
$17.0 million

Texas Commerce[a]
$ 5.1 million

Total Capitalization
$55.8 million

Austin

Venture Capital Partnerships

Business Development Partners
$10.4 million

Firm										
Rotan Mosie Technology Partners	X	—	X	—	—	—	—	—	—	—
Allied Bancshares Capital	X	X	X	X	X	X	X	X	X	X
American Energy Investment	—	—	—	—	X	—	—	—	—	—
Bow Lane Capital	X	X	X	—	X	X	—	X	—	—
Charter Venture Group	—	—	—	—	X	—	—	—	—	X
Energy Capital	—	—	—	—	X	—	—	—	—	—
Evergreen Capital	—	—	—	—	—	X	X	—	X	—
Red River Ventures	—	—	—	—	X	—	—	—	—	—
SBI Capital	X	X	X	—	X	—	—	—	—	X
Texas Capital	X	—	X	—	X	X	—	—	—	—
Texas Commerce	X	X	X	—	X	—	X	X	—	X
Business Development Partners	—	—	—	X	X	—	—	—	—	—

Table A–4 continued

	Computer Related	Robotics	Medical	Tele-communications	Manu-facturing	Oil and Gas Related	Semi-Conductor	Broad-casting	Food Service	Other
SBICs										
FSA Capital $31.95 million	X	—	—	X	—	X	—	—	—	X
Rust Capital $35.0 million	X	—	X	X	X	—	—	X	—	X
Total Capitalization $77.35 million										
San Antonio										
Venture Capital Partnerships										
Hixon/Southwest Venture Partners $74.5 million	X	—	X	X	X	—	—	X	—	—
SBICs										
Cameron Financial $ 0.5 million	—	—	—	—	—	—	—	—	—	—
San Antonio Venture Group $ 1.0 million	—	—	—	—	—	—	—	—	—	—
Total Capitalization $76.0 million										

aDenotes a bank subsidiary.

Table A-5
Selected Venture Investment Institutions: Investment by State

Dallas

	AL	AK	AR	CA	CO	FL	GA	IL	IN	KS	MA	MI	MS	NC	NH	NM	NY	OH	OK	OR	PA	TN	TX	UT	VA	DC
Venture Capital Partnerships																										
Capital Southwest $ 37.2 million	—	—	—	—	—	—	—	—	—	—	—	—	—	—	—	—	—	—	—	—	—	—	—	—	—	—
Barry Cash $ 25.0 million	—	—	—	X	X	—	—	—	—	X	X	X	—	—	—	—	—	—	X	—	—	—	X	—	—	—
MSI Capital Capitalization Unavailable	—	—	—	—	—	—	—	—	—	—	—	—	—	—	—	—	—	—	—	—	—	—	X	—	—	—
Southwest Enterprise Associates $ 25.0 million	—	—	—	—	—	—	—	—	—	—	—	—	—	—	—	—	—	—	—	—	—	—	X	—	—	—
Sunwestern Investment $ 11.7 million	X	X	—	—	—	—	—	X	—	—	—	—	—	—	—	—	—	—	—	—	—	—	X	—	—	—
Sevin Rosen $ 85.0 million	—	—	—	X	X	—	—	—	—	—	X	—	—	—	—	—	—	—	—	X	—	—	X	—	—	—
Texas Venture Partners $ 15.0 million	—	—	—	X	—	—	—	—	—	—	—	—	—	—	X	—	—	—	—	—	—	—	X	—	—	—
SBICs																										
Brittany Capital $ 0.5 million	—	—	—	—	—	—	—	—	—	—	—	X	—	—	—	—	—	—	—	—	—	—	X	—	—	—
Commerce Southwest Capital[a] $ 1.0 million	—	—	—	—	—	—	X	—	—	—	—	—	X	—	—	—	—	—	—	—	—	—	X	—	—	—
Interfirst Venture[a] $ 12.5 million	—	—	—	—	—	—	X	—	—	—	X	—	—	—	—	—	—	—	X	—	—	—	X	X	—	—
MESBIC of Dallas $ 2.0 million	—	—	—	—	—	—	—	—	—	—	—	—	—	—	—	—	—	—	—	—	—	—	—	X	—	—
Republic Venture Group[a] $ 12.0 million	X	—	—	X	X	—	—	—	—	—	X	—	—	—	—	—	—	—	X	—	—	—	X	X	—	—

Total Capitalization $266.9 million

Table A–5 continued

	AL	AK	AR	CA	CO	FL	GA	IL	IN	KS	MA	MI	MS	NC	NH	NM	NY	OH	OK	OR	PA	TN	TX	UT	VA	DC
Houston																										
Venture Capital Partnerships																										
Rotan Mosle Technology Partners $ 3.2 million	—	—	—	X	X	—	—	—	—	—	—	—	—	—	—	—	—	—	—	—	—	—	X	—	—	—
SBICs																										
Allied Bancshares Capital[a] $11.7 million	—	—	—	—	—	X	—	—	—	X	—	—	—	—	—	X	—	—	—	—	—	—	X	—	—	—
American Energy Investment $ 2.5 million	—	—	—	—	—	—	—	—	—	—	—	—	—	—	—	—	—	—	X	—	—	—	X	—	—	—
Bow Lane Capital $ 2.5 million	—	—	—	X	—	—	—	—	—	—	—	—	—	—	—	—	X	—	—	X	—	X	X	—	—	—
Charter Venture Group[a] $ 3.0 million	—	—	—	—	—	—	—	—	—	—	—	—	—	—	—	—	—	—	—	—	—	—	X	—	—	—
Energy Capital $12.0 million	—	—	—	—	—	—	—	—	—	—	—	—	—	—	—	—	—	—	—	—	—	—	X	—	—	—
Evergreen Capital $ 2.0 million	—	—	—	—	—	X	—	X	—	—	X	—	—	—	—	—	—	—	—	—	—	—	X	—	—	X
Red River Ventures Capitalization Unavailable	—	—	—	—	—	—	—	—	—	—	—	—	—	—	—	—	—	—	—	—	—	—	X	—	—	—
SBI Capital $ 1.0 million	—	—	—	X	—	—	—	—	—	—	—	—	—	—	—	—	—	X	X	—	—	—	X	—	—	—
Texas Capital $17.0 million	X	—	—	X	X	—	—	—	—	—	—	—	—	—	—	—	—	—	—	—	—	—	X	—	X	—
Texas Commerce[a] $10.0 million	—	—	—	X	—	—	—	X	—	—	X	—	—	—	—	—	—	—	—	—	—	—	X	—	—	—
Total Capitalization $61.7 million																										

Austin

Venture Capital Partnerships
Business Development Partners
$10.4 million

SBICs
FSA Capital
$31.95 million
Rust Capital
$35.0 million

Total Capitalization
$77.35 million

San Antonio

Venture Capital Partnerships
Hixon/Southwest Venture
Partners
$74.5 million

SBICs
Cameron Financial
$ 0.5 million
San Antonio Venture Group
$ 1.0 million

Total Capitalization
$76.0 million

aDenotes bank subsidiary.

Table A-6
Directory of Investments by Selected Venture Institutions

Venture Institution	Type of Industry	Company Invested In	Type of Investment
1. Allied Bancshare *Capital Corporation* SBIC since 1979 Wholly owned subsidiary of Allied Bancshares Located in Houston Capitalization: $11.7 million	Chemicals	Allco Chemical Corp. Galena, KS	Participated in $9 million leveraged buyout financing
	Communications	Hess Broadcasting Co. Pensacola, FL	Sole investor in leveraged buyout financing
		Quest Microwave Dallas, TX	Sole venture capital investor, has provided two stages of financing
	Oil and Gas	Texas Supply Corp. Odessa, TX	Sole venture capital investor in an expansion-stage financing
	Robotics	Automated Robotic Systems, Inc. Arlington, TX	Leveraged buyout, $1.6 million participation
	Transportation	Railtex, Inc. San Antonio, TX	Sole venture capital investor, Investment unavailable.
2. *American Energy Investment, Inc.* SBIC since 1981 Privately held Located in Houston Manages $2.5 million	Oil and Gas Midland, TX	High Plains Exploration	$4 million capital venture financing, $2 million bank financing, $6 million total
		National Tubular Systems Tulsa, OK	Participated in $4 million financing
		Sere Corporation Houston, TX	Oil and gas exploration; lead financier, $600,000

3. *Barry Cash Southwest Partnership*
Venture capital partnership since 1983
Located in Dallas
Manages $25 million

	Soltex Oil and Gas, Dallas, TX	Participated in $8 million second-stage financing
Computers	Convex Computer Corp. Richardson, TX	Designs and manufactures high-performance scientific computers; participated in a $16 million second-stage financing
	Intelligence Storage, Inc. Longmont, CO	Manufactures high performance peripheral controllers, participated in a $4.5 million start-up financing
	Silicon Graphics, Inc. Mountain View, CA	Manufactures graphics terminals and work stations; participated in a $16.7 million bridge financing
Communications	Zaisan Corp. Houston, TX	Manufactures an integrated voice/data work station; participated in a $10 million second-stage financing

4. *Bow Lane Capital Corporation*
SBIC since 1980
Located in Houston
Manages $2.5 million

Communications	Dalsat, Inc. Plano, TX	Earth station manufacturer; investment unavailable
	Venus Scientific, Inc.	TV cameras and power supplies; investment unavailable
Computer Systems	Digital Pathways, Inc. Palo Alto, CA	Participated in a $1 million first-stage financing
	Mathews Corp. Hillsboro, OR	Manufactures color graphics controllers and work stations; participated in a $11.5 million first-stage financing

Table A-6 continued

Venture Institution	Type of Industry	Company Invested In	Type of Investment
		Numeric Micro Corp. Dallas, TX	Computer Systems for machine tool users; investment unavailable
	Medical Equipment	Life Science Instrumentation, Inc. Portland, OR	Led a $650,000 first-stage financing
	Oil Patch Communications	Drilling Information Service Corporation Houston, TX	Sole institutional investor; early-stage financing; investment unavailable
	Robotics	Advanced Manufacturing Systems, Inc. Houston, TX	Participated in a $1.3 million second-stage financing
	Semiconductors	California Microdevices Sunnyvale, CA	Investment unavailable
		Morgan Semiconductor Garland, TX	Gallium arsenide semiconductors; leveraged buyout and expansion financing, lead investor, $475,000 financing
	Software	Test Systems Strategies, Inc. Beaverton, OR	Sole investor in a first-stage financing, investment unavailable
5. *Brittany Capital Corporation* SBIC since 1969 Located in Dallas Capitalization: $500,000	Cable TV	Lamar Cable Partners Jackson, MS	Investment unavailable
	Oil Field Services	Diagnostic Services Dallas, TX	Technological approach to solving oil field problems; Brittany-originated start-up financing, amount unavailable

6. Business Development Partners

Capital venture partnership since 1981

Focuses on early-stage technology-related companies

Located in Austin, branch office in Dallas

$11.4 million

Restaurant	Chili's Dallas, TX	Planning an IPO; investment unavailable
Miscellaneous	Precept, Inc. Dallas, TX	Investment originated and later sold to G.D. Searle, investment unavailable
Biotechnology	Advanced Mineral Technologies, Inc. Socorro, NM	Microbial waste water clean-up and precious metal recovery; $1 million seed financing
Communications	Telamco Corporation Charlotte, NC	Alternate long distance telephone company; participated in starting financing of $1.2 million
	Photophone San Antonio, TX	The photophone captures and transmits single frame images over voice grade phone lines at high speed; participated in seed and first-round $2M financing
	Advanced Business Communications Dallas, TX	Digital switch manufacturer; participated in $2M first-round financing
Computers	Compupsych Kansas City, KS	Computerized testing, software for psychologists; sole institutional investor, early stage financing, investment unavailable
	Micro Peripherals Salt Lake City, UT	Dot matrix printers; early investor, later participated in a $1.1 million financing
	Validec, Inc. San Francisco, CA	Proprietary hardware and software systems for the hospitality industry; participant in $400K seed and later $2.3M first-round financing

Table A-6 continued

Venture Institution	Type of Industry	Company Invested In	Type of Investment
	Space Technology	Orbital Sciences Corp. Washington, DC	Company has agreement with NASA to develop and privately operate payload modules to transport satellites from space shuttle to GEO; provided initial $1.8M financing
7. *Capital Southwest Corporation* Business development company since 1961 Located in Dallas Net asset value: $39.6 million	Biotechnology	Repligen Corp. Cambridge, MA	Invested $300,200 in a $5.7 million start-up financing
	Communications	International Signal and Control	Investment unavailable
		U.S. Telephone Dallas, TX	Long distance carrier; has invested $805,000 in a $8.2 million financing
		Lexitel Corp. Birmingham, MI	Long distance telephone network; invested $1.25 million in a $16.4 million first-stage financing
	Manufactured Housing	Oak Creek Homes, Inc. Dallas, TX	Invested $750,000 in a $2 million second-stage financing
		Palm Harbor Homes, Inc.	Investment unavailable
	Oil and Gas	Alamo Group	Steel castings
		Gulf Energy and Development	$575,000 investment

	Hercules Offshore Drilling	Workover services, $730,000 investment
Other	American Nursery Products Tahlequah, OK	Invested $675,000 in expansion financing
	Columbia Scientific Industries Corp. Austin, TX	Manufactures laboratory instruments; $150,000 first-stage investment
	Abek, Inc. Colorado Springs, CO	Electron beam lithography for semiconductor manufacture; $240,000 investment in first-stage financing
	Varix Corp. Richardson, TX	Manufactures memory and programming equipment; participated in a $1 million first-stage financing.

8. *Charter Venture Group, Inc.*
SBIC since 1980
Charter Bankshares, Inc. subsidiary
Located in Houston
Manages $1 million

Biotechnology	Hyclone, Inc. Conroe, TX	Agricultural biotechnology; participated in a $700,000 first-stage financing
Oil and Gas	Houston Oil Fields Co. Houston, TX	Participated in an $8.6 million expansion financing
	Realm Resources, Inc. Houston, TX	Participated in a $9.6 million expansion financing
Robotics	Automated Robotic Systems, Inc. Arlington, TX	Participated in leveraged buyout $1.6 million
Other	Southpoint Porsche Audi Houston, TX	Sole institutional investor in a leveraged buyout

Table A-6 continued

Venture Institution	Type of Industry	Company Invested In	Type of Investment
9. *Commerce Southwest Capital* SBIC since 1981 BancTexas Dallas subsidiary Private capital: $1 million	Oil and Gas	Endevco, Inc. Dallas, TX	Natural gas processing; investment unavailable
		American Well Servicing Dallas, TX	Investment unavailable
10. *Curtin and Company, Inc./ Red River Ventures, Inc.* Partnership/SBIC since 1974 Located in Houston Total capital under management unavailable, SBIC manages private capital: $751,000 SBA leverage: $1,800,000	Oil and Gas	Modrill, Inc.	Workover rigs; Red River provided $150,000 start-up financing, other participated
		Superior Hydraulics, Inc.	Oil field equipment; provided $100,000 of $500,000 financing
11. *Evergreen Capital* SBIC since 1979 Located in Houston Manages $2 million	Broadcast Communications	American Cable Systems Boston, MA	$397,000 investment in second-stage financing
		GRB Communications, Inc. Dallas, TX	Provided $385,000 of $700,000, financing led by Evergreen
		King's Bay Cable Vision, Inc. St. Mary's, GA	$360,000 of $550,000 financing participation
	Publishing	Airline Publishing Group Washington, DC	Lead investor, provided half of a $500,000 financing
	Utilities	Atlantic Utilities Corp. Miami, FL	Provided $267,500 of $749,000 of venture capital
	Manufacturing	Heico, Inc. Chicago, IL	Provided $325,000 of a $5.8 million leveraged buyout

12. FSA Capital, Ltd.
SBIC since 1982
Located in Austin
Manages $1.95 million
Founded Triad Ventures, a $30 million partnership in late 1984

Industry	Company	Details
Food Service	TGIF, Texas Dallas, TX	Restaurants; $275,000 of $725,000 financing participation
Oil and Gas	DWS Energy Charlotte, TX	Well Servicing; expansion financing participation, $1.34 million
	Solids International Waco, TX	Cleaning of drilling fluids; sole investor, $1.2 million financing
	Texas Gas Transport Austin, TX	Participated in $3.3 million financing
Communications	Near Space Communications Plano, TX	Raised $2.25 million for development financing
	U.S. Telephone	Long distance resale common carrier; $8.2 million financing
Computer-Related	Cyb Systems Austin, TX	Manufactures a super microcomputer; participated in a $4.5 million expansion financing
	Nova Graphics International Corp. Austin, TX	Formed a $900,000 partnership to finance product development
Publishing	New England Monthly Haydenville, MA	Raised $3.3 million for a private placement

13. InterFirst Venture Corporation
SBIC since 1961
InterFirst Bank subsidiary
Located in Dallas
Manages $12.5 million private capital plus $9.5 leveraged capital with SBA

Industry	Company	Details
Oil and Gas	Hrubetz Petroleum Corp. Dallas, TX	IFVC sold venture investor, investment unavailable
	Tescorp, Inc. San Antonio, TX	Oil field service; investment unavailable
	Titan Rig Tulsa, OK	Investment unavailable

Table A-6 continued

Venture Institution	Type of Industry	Company Invested In	Type of Investment
	Broadcasting	American Cablesystems Boston, MA	Investment unavailable
		Prime Cable Corp. Austin, TX	Investment unavailable
		Civic Communications Jackson, MS	Sole investor in a leveraged buy-out, investment unavailable
	Medical	Surgicare Corp. Houston, TX	Outpatient surgery centers; participated in $4 million start-up financing
	Food Service	D'Lites of America Norcross, GA	$2 million participation
		European Bakers Tucker, GA	$1 million participation
	Communications	Optical Data Systems Richardson, TX	Participated in a first stage expansion financing, investment unavailable
	Retail	Storehouse, Inc. Atlanta, GA	Sole investor in a leveraged buyout
	Semiconductors	Semiconductor Test Technologies, Inc. Honey Grove, TX	Sole investor in an expansion financing
		Varix Corporation Richardson, TX	Led a $1 million first-stage financing
	Software	The Rand Group Addison, TX	Sole investor in a first-stage financing, investment unavailable

14. MESBIC Financial Corp. of Dallas
MESBIC since 1970
Located in Dallas
Private capitalization: $2 million

Other	Flight America Lynchburg, VA	Charter air services
	TEI Fluid Power Arlington, TX	Hydraulic components; sole investor, $1 million acquisition
Technology-Related	Moreno Group Richardson and Dallas, TX	Printed circuit boards; led $600,000 financing, obtained $1.25 million debt
Food Service	Ninfas Restaurants Dallas, TX	Investment unavailable
Oil and Gas	Star/Adair Insulation Odessa, TX	Oil field service; investment unavailable

15. MSI Capital Corporation
Venture capital partnership since 1976
Located in Dallas
Private capitalization amount unavailable

Communications	Near Space Communications Dallas, TX	PBX equipment; lead financing and start-up investment, participated in financings of $500,000 and $2.25 million
Other	Able Enterprises Ennis, TX	Custom van windows provided funds for company's takeover
	Forms Systems, Inc.	Specialty business forms; only institutional investor, provided seed financing, investment unavailable

16. Republic Venture Group
SBIC since 1961
Republic National Bank subsidiary
Located in Dallas
Manages $8.3 million

Oil and Gas	Maze Exploration, Inc. Denver, CO	$1 million financing participant
Semiconductors	International Microelectronics Products San Jose, CA	MOS integrated circuits; $5.6 million first-stage participation

Table A-6 continued

Venture Institution	Type of Industry	Company Invested In	Type of Investment
	Medical	Care Medical Products, Inc. Huntsville, AL	Patient monitoring systems; participated in $1 million financing
		Ambulatory Hospitals of America Houston, TX	Participated in an $11.9 million first-stage financing
		Pharmacy Practice Group Dallas, TX	Participated in a $2 million second-stage financing
	Communications	RF Monolithics, Inc. Dallas, TX	Participated in second-stage financing, investment unavailable
		Lexitel Corp. Birmingham, MI	Participated in a $16.4 million first-stage financing
	Computer-Related	Cadmus Computer Systems Lowell, MA	Participated in a $9 million first-stage financing
	Manufacturing	Monarch Paint Co. Houston, TX	Participated in a $1.4 million leveraged buyout
	Software	Digital Research, Inc. Pacific Grove, CA	Participated in a $17 million bridge financing
17. *Rotan Mosle Technology Partners* Venture capital partnership since 1983 Invests on a side-by-side basis with Taylor and Turner, San Francisco Located in Houston Over $3 million in investments to date, total capital size unavailable	Computer-Related	Akashic Memories Corp. Santa Clara, CA	Participated in a $2.4 million second-stage financing
	Software	TCS Software Houston, TX	Participated in a $1 million expansion financing
		Consillium Associates Palo Alto, CA	Participated in a $1.1 million first-stage financing

Category	Company	Description
Biotechnology	Oncor, Inc. Gaithersburg, MD	Participated in a $700,000 start-up financing
Communications	Photophone Company, Inc. San Antonio, TX	Participated in a $2.1 million first-stage financing
Retailing	The Genra Group Dallas, TX	Participated in a leveraged buy-out, amount unavailable
Broadcast Communication	Apple Broadcasting Siloam Springs, AR	FM radio station; participated in leveraged buyout of $500,000
	Chrysostom Corporation	VHF TV station; sole investor, expansion financing, investment unavailable
Communications	Dalsat, Inc. Plano, TX	Participated in a $1.8 million second-stage financing
	Rostra Holdings, Inc. Alliance, OH	Specialty aluminum equipment; led a leveraged buyout of $600,000
	Rubo Enterprises El Monte, CA	Paperboard mounts; leveraged buyout without partners, $700,000
Medical	H & M Laboratory Services Boston, MA	Dental laboratory business; led a $2.6 million leveraged buyout
Software	Concentric Data Systems, Inc. Westboro, MA	Participated in a $3.2 million second-stage financing
Other	American Cable Systems Boston, MA	TGIF Texas, Fort Worth, Texas restaurants; follow-up financings, investment unavailable

18. *Rust Capital, Ltd.*
   SBIC since 1979
   Located in Austin
   Manages $7 million private capital, $2.8 million SBA leverage
   Founded Rust Venture partners in late 1984, $28 million capitalization

Table A-6 continued

Venture Institution	Type of Industry	Company Invested In	Type of Investment
19. *SBIC Capital Corporation* SBIC since 1981 Located in Houston Capitalized at $1 million	Oil and Gas	Amicor, Inc. Tulsa, OK	Stand-by generators; participated in a $3.5 million financing
		Fabricated Systems International Katy, TX	Seamless tubing; participated in $15 million financing
		Sunnybrook Oil & Gas Tyler, TX	Oil and gas exploration; $4 million second-stage participation
		Houston Oil Fields Co. Houston, TX	Participated in an $8.6 million private placement
		Plains Resources, Inc. Oklahoma City, OK	Participated in a $6 million second-stage financing
	Computer-Related	Capro, Inc. Garden Grove, CA	Software company; participated in first-stage financing of $3 million
	Robotics	Advanced Manufacturing Systems, Inc. Houston, TX	Participated in a $1.3 million second-stage financing
	Medical-Related	Exidyne, Inc. Colorado Springs, CO	Led a $275,000 second-stage financing
	Service	Texas First Brokerage Services, Inc. Houston, TX	Participated in a $1.6 million start-up financing

20. Seven Rosen Management Company
Venture capital partnership
Initial funding 1981, second funding 1983
$25 million initial pool, $60 million second pool

Computers	Synapse Corp. San Francisco, CA	Investment amount unavailable
	Silicon Graphics, Inc. Mountain View, CA	Investment amount unavailable
	Amcodyne, Inc. Denver, CO	Investment amount unavailable
	Parsee Scientific Computer Corp. Dallas, TX	Investment amount unavailable
	Compaq Computer Houston, TX	Investment amount unavailable
	Osborne Computer Santa Clara, CA	Investment amount unavailable
	Northwest Instrument Systems Portland, OR	Investment amount unavailable
	Cadtek Corp. Santa Clara, CA	Investment amount unavailable
	Landmark Graphics Corp. Houston, TX	Investment amount unavailable
Computer-Related	Enmasse Computer Corp. Acton, MA	Participated in a $3.5 million start-up financing

Table A-6 continued

Venture Institution	Type of Industry	Company Invested In	Type of Investment
		General Parametrics Berkeley, CA	Participated in a $2.5 million start-up financing
		Proteon, Inc. Natick, MA	Participated in a $2.4 million expansion financing
		The Palantir Corp. Santa Clara, CA	Participated in a $4 million start-up financing
	Software	Lotus Development Corp. Boston, MA	Investment amount unavailable
		Electronic Arts Santa Clara, CA	Investment amount unavailable
		Computer Thought Plano, TX	Investment amount unavailable
		Quarterdeck Office Systems Santa Monica, CA	Participated in a $5.8 million start-up financing
	Semiconductors	Cypress Semiconductor Corp. Santa Clara, CA	Investment amount unavailable
		Emulogic, Inc. Westwood, MA	Investment amount unavailable
	Medical Technology	Intelledex, Inc. Corvallis, OR	Investment amount unavailable
		Acuson San Francisco, CA	Investment amount unavailable

21. *Southwest Enterprise Associates*

Venture capital partnership since 1983
Located in Dallas
Manages $25 million

Industry	Company	Investment
Communications	Pronet, Inc. Addison, TX	Investment amount unavailable
Communications	Menlo Corp. Santa Clara, CA	Participated in a $3.6 million second-stage financing
Communications	Shared Resource Exchange, Inc. Dallas, TX	PBX manufacturer; participated in a $2.5 million second-stage financing
	Zarsan Corp. Houston, TX	Participated in a $10 million second-stage financing
Computer-Related	Convex Computer Corp. Richardson, TX	Participated in a $16 million second-stage financing
Semiconductor	Dallas Semiconductor Corp. Dallas, TX	Participated in a $2 million start-up financing
Software	TCS Software Houston, TX	Participated in a $1 million expansion financing

22. *Southwest Venture Partners/ HixVen Partners*

Southwest Venture Partners— Capital venture firm since 1975
Located in San Antonio with offices in Dallas
Manages 3 pools—$12.0 million, $20 million, and $42.5 million

Industry	Company	Investment
Computer	Via Systems, Inc. North Billerica, MA	Participated in a $4.3 million second-stage financing
	Cadmus Computer Systems, Inc. Lowell, MA	Participated in a $9 million first-stage financing
	Scott Systems, Inc. Southborough, MA	Airline reservation terminals and computers; participated in $3.2 million financing, $800,000 from Southwest Venture Partners

Table A-6 continued

Venture Institution	Type of Industry	Company Invested In	Type of Investment
		Ferix Corporation Sunnyvale, CA	Non-impact printing; $300,000 investment
		Electronics Systems Products, Inc. Titusville, FL	Color video projectors; investment unavailable, follow-on financing
	Communications	Photophone, Ltd. San Antonio, TX	Led a $2 million start-up financing
		Communications Office Machines Denver, CO	Participated in a $2.4 million start-up financing
		VMX Inc. Richardson, TX	Voice message retrieval: follow-on investment, investment unavailable
		Commterm, Inc. Hingham, MA	Voice message storage and retrieval; investment unavailable
	Manufacturing	Alrexchange, Inc. Hingham, MA	Sole institutional investor, investment unavailable
	Medical	Infomed Corp. Englewood, CO	Participated in a $4.2 million second-stage financing
		Oncolab, Inc. Santa Clara, CA	Participated in a $1.5 million start-up financing
		Bio Diagnostics, Inc. Arlington, TX	Blood serum agents; follow-on investment, amount unavailable
		Medical 21 Corp. Dallas, TX	Free-standing surgical centers; follow-on investment, amount unavailable

23. *Sunwestern Investment Fund*
Venture capital partnership since 1981
Located in Dallas
Manages $9 million

Category	Company	Description
Software	Shared Financial Systems, Inc. Dallas, TX	Participated in a $1.5 million third-stage financing
Other	Polymer Technology Corp. Wilmington, MA	Manufactures gas-permeable contact lens
Oil and Gas	Baker North Slope Wireline Service Co. Anchorage, AL	Participated in a $2.4 million start-up financing
Communications	Promet, Inc. Dallas, TX	Radio paging service; participated in a $2 million second-stage financing
Semiconductors	Drexler Technology Corp.	Invested in this public company, investment unavailable
	Microdynamics, Inc. Dallas, TX	Participated in a $2.5 million second-stage financing
Manufacturing	Continental Water Systems Corp. San Antonio, TX	Industrial water purifiers; participated in a $4.3 million leveraged buyout
Software	Computerose, Inc. Arlington, TX	Sole investor in a start-up financing, investment unavailable
	Lantech Systems, Inc. Dallas, TX	Participated in a $1.5 million second-stage financing
	Shared Financial Systems, Inc. Dallas, TX	Participated in a $1.5 million first-stage financing
Medical-Related	Kyoto Diagnostics Elkhart, IN	Participated in a $3.3 million start-up financing

Table A-6 continued

Venture Institution	Type of Industry	Company Invested In	Type of Investment
24. *Texas Capital Corporation/ Texas Capital Venture Investments Corporation* TCC is an SBIC, TCVIC an unregulated investments corporation Founded in 1959 Located in Houston Manages $17 million	Medical	Care Medical Products, Inc. Huntsville, AL	Patient monitoring systems; participated in a $1 million expansion financing
	Manufacturing	Catalytic Damper Corporation Flint Hill, VA	Exhaust systems; participated in start-up financing of $200,000
		Marlin Lewis, Inc. Dallas, TX	Wood lattice manufacturer; sole investor in $270,000 third-stage financing
		Quail Plastics Dallas, TX	PVC pipe; leverged buyout, sole institutional participation, investment unavailable
	Oil and Gas	Venna Corporation Houston, TX	Invested in this public electricity and power oil company, investment unavailable
	Semiconductors	Abek, Inc. Colorado Springs, CO	Follow-on investment in this lithography, investment unavailable
25. *Texas Commerce Investment Co.* SBIC since 1982 Texas Commerce Bank subsidiary Located in Houston Manages $5.1 million	Computer-Related	Sunrise Systems, Inc. Dallas, TX	Leveraged buyout, sole investor, amount unavailable; brought to them by parent bank
		Cadmus Computer Systems, Inc. Lowell, MA	Participated in a $9 million first-stage financing

26. *Texas Venture Partners 1984 Ltd./ Lexington Venture Partners 1983, Ltd.*

Venture capital partnership since 1983

Located in Dallas

Manages $15 million

Industry	Company	Financing
Robotics	Automated Robotic Systems, Inc. Arlington, TX	Participated in a $1.6 million leveraged buyout
Medical-Related	Ambulatory Hospitals of America Houston, TX	Participated in a $11.9 million second-stage financing
	Orange Medical Instruments, Inc. Costa Mesa, CA	Participated in a $3.5 million second-stage financing
Broadcasting	Combined Cable Corp. Chicago, IL	Participated in a $3 million third-stage financing
Oil and Gas	Houston Oil Fields Co. Houston, TX	Participated in a $8.6 million expansion financing
Biotechnology	Hyclone, Inc. Conroe, TX	Participated in a $700,000 first-stage financing
Service	Equus Capital Corp. Houston, TX	Leveraged buyout fund; participated in a $6.5 million first-stage financing
Computer-Related	Personal Peripherals, Inc. Dallas, TX	Participated in a start-up financing, amount unavailable
	Speech Plus, Inc. Mountain View, CA	Participated in a $3.5 million start-up financing
Semiconductors	Environmental Processing, Inc. Dallas, TX	Provided expansion financing, amount unavailable

Table A-6 continued

Venture Institution	Type of Industry	Company Invested In	Type of Investment
	Communications	Davox Communication Corp. Merrimack, NH	Participated in a $4.1 million second-stage financing
		Tekton Industries, Inc. Dallas, TX	Participated in $4.7 million of first- and expansion-stage financing

Appendix B:
Key Elements of a Business Plan

To establish a successful venture-backed company, an entrepreneur must maneuver his or her company through separate phases of business development, none of which may be initiated before the prior stage is completed. When a concept for a technologically advanced product is complete, the first question an entrepreneur must ask is not whether its production is technically feasible or whether financing is available, but whether a market for the product exists. If there is no market, there can be no company.

To attract venture capital financing, a business plan is essential. It would be difficult to overstate the importance of the business plan in the quest for venture capital. The business plan is useful, not just to venture capitalists, but also to bankers, accounting firms, lawyers, and to people who simply want to sit down and know more about the company so that they can do a better job of providing it with some sort of service. While the business plan is extremely important, it does not have to be long or complicated. It can even be simple. The purpose is to tell, in as straightforward a manner as possible, the following:

1. what the idea is;
2. who you are and why you think you can implement this idea, including perhaps a resume and background;
3. who else is required to achieve the objective;
4. how the market will develop; and
5. what the ultimate numbers will look like.

The business plan is often the only avenue open for the entrepreneur to convince the venture capitalist that the idea is worthy of backing. In a typical venture capital pool, a minimum of 600 other business plans are competing for the venture capitalist's attention and funds. Consequently, the aspiring entrepreneur must tailor the business plan to give the venture capitalist every reason to read and consider seriously his idea.

An effective business plan follows a few basic rules. First, it must be concise: this means it must be short and to the point, while remaining complete. Second, the business plan must provide ready access to the information the venture capitalist requires to make his assessment: this information includes, but is not limited to, critical variables such as anticipated financial information, managerial resumes, and marketing projections. Finally, it should contain an analysis of the entrepreneur's market, market niche, and future growth potential of the entrepreneur's venture. While there is no set formula for a good business plan, most contain the following sections.

Executive Summary

This section serves primarily to highlight the strengths of the business proposal. It should not be a rehash of the table of contents. Critical information for this section includes:

1. the purpose of the business plan, that is, to raise capital;
2. a brief description of the product or service;
3. an outline of the market size and a description of the segment of the market one plans to enter;
4. product development milestones;
5. a summary of key financial ratios, milestones, and projected income flows;
6. an estimate of the amount of venture capital the firm requires, and the uses to which the funds will be put; and
7. a brief description of the management team and their experience in the fields where they will work.

A well-written executive summary allows prospective investors to decide quickly whether the plan deserves further study. In addition, it can quickly narrow the search for venture capital to those venture capitalists truly interested in the industry. It can also be mailed in place of a full business plan, thereby minimizing search costs and limiting the distribution of proprietary ideas. Interested parties can then be given the full business plan.

Table of Contents

The organization of the business plan into clearly defined sections enables the reader to locate specific areas of interest. In the case of many venture capital partnerships, persons with different areas of expertise will read various parts of the plan and the table of contents will facilitate each reviewer's task.

Organization and Management

This section should serve as a general overview of the company's product or service, its market niche, and the organizational structure with which the company intends to penetrate the market. Leaving the detailed description of the product and markets for other sections, the discussion of these topics here sets the stage for the introduction of the enterprise's management team. The management team is usually the first filter the venture capitalist employs in selecting among potential investments. In the venture capital industry, the opinion is commonly voiced that money is invested not in ideas, but in people. To impress upon the venture capitalist the viability of the idea and the management team to implement it, the business plan should detail how the company will be organized, who will fill each position, and what responsibilities each position will have. The weaknesses as well as the strengths of the management team should be analyzed so the venture capitalist sees where the individual talents of the management team lend synergy to the organization and where the management team will need strengthening to make a successful venture. Such a critical analysis lends credibility to the venture. Furthermore, one of the strengths a venture capitalist brings to a portfolio company is his network of associates in industry that comprises an excellent management-locating service.

In this section, detailed resumes are not necessary. Complete resumes of all key management personnel should be in an appendix where the venture capitalist can study them. Included in the resume should be employment information (including company, position, responsibilities, dates, and reasons for leaving), educational information, and all relevant addresses of references at these institutions so that the venture capitalist can thoroughly check the manager's background; the venture capitalist will definitely check references.

Background and History

This section is optional. It should comprise a short history of the development of the product line or of the identification of the unique business opportunity. Depending on the technology being readied for marketing, a summary of the development of technological progress in the field is pertinent. This helps the investor place the product in perspective.

Product Strategy

In a concise and nontechnical manner, the business plan should present a description of the product and explain how that product will be put into production. This product description need not be highly detailed, for the investor need not appreciate the fine points of design work unless they comprise a significant market advantage. What will interest the venture capitalist are the features of the product or service which materially benefit the ultimate customer by virtue of productivity or unique application.

If a prototype of the product to be manufactured has already been developed, the business plan should contain a photograph of it. If no prototype exists, a theoretical diagram of the product is appropriate. If there is a proprietary technology in the product, this should be noted, and if the product is a unique application of existing technology, then the holders of licensable patents should be listed. Beyond the present product, the potential for new products stemming from this technology should be listed. Future earnings from the present product line must be supplemented within a few years if the venture is to continue revenue and earnings growth later on. Furthermore, the business plan should explain what distinctive competence the company possesses in the field that enables it to be competitive technologically.

Research and development is a consideration that can be discussed under product strategy or that can be made into a separate section, depending on the importance of the subject to the ultimate success of the venture. The discussion should address the current status of the product's technology (that is, concept, prototype, near or in production); what elements of the product are patented or patentable; what extent of development is necessary to reach a patentable and produceable stage; who has the ability within the company to perform the proprietary research and development; what companies have the technological skill and capacity to compete on a technological level with the proposed venture; what the technological status of future products is currently; how much money will be allocated to research and development; and what the germane risks are concerning this technological field. Specifically, the risks that should be detailed include technological obsolescence, market obsolescence, and regulatory constraints. The costs for all the research and development should be forecast with key milestones, targets, and probable bottlenecks identified.

Market Analysis and Marketing Strategy

Venture capitalists understand markets and marketing. Very likely they will have a feel for the market which a prospective entrepreneur intends to enter, since venture capitalists are increasingly targeting specific markets for investment. This section is one of the most important in the business plan. The ability to market a product or service will ultimately determine whether the venture is a success.

The section should start with an analysis of the industry and its outlook. The present size of the market and market projections should be detailed for five years and possibly for ten years. The major users of the industry's product should be broken out, and the major trends among these customers' usage patterns should be explored. Next, the market should be quantified by segment. Segments can be defined by price range, by application, by technological sophistication, or by a combination of these factors.

The second part of this section should deal with the targeted market niche that the company's prospective product will enter. Careful market segmentation is important for accurate market penetration projections, and the entrepreneur writing the business plan should take great care not to overstate his market penetration projections. Venture capitalists will probably reject a proposal that projects a 50 percent market share for a new or start-up company since such a projection is, from experience, highly unrealistic. The entrepreneur should also present an analysis of the profitability of the various market segments to support his or her entry into a particular segment.

Competition in the targeted industry is of such great importance to the prospective investor that it should comprise a third part of this section. The business plan should list current competitors by market niche and by market share. In addition, potential competitors who may be planning to enter the market or who are likely to enter the market due to technological compatibility should be identified. A useful tactic to estimate the competitiveness of the product relative to others currently on the market is to solicit customer reactions to the product or service, and list the positive and negative points from their perspective.

Finally, the business plan should identify the marketing and distribution activities the firm plans to undertake. In this regard, the business plan should answer questions concerning distribution channels, service networks, warranty considerations, pricing policies, geographical market penetration strategy (including, if applicable, international markets and distribution), customer identification techniques, advertising and public relations philosophy, and costs associated with these factors.

In this section consistent attention should be paid to the documentation of facts and figures. Few investors take at face value an entrepreneur's estimates since the entrepreneur tends to be highly enthusiastic about his idea and usually does not have the expertise to forecast such variables.

Production and Manufacturing

Manufacturing the product is an important consideration for the prospective entrepreneur, especially since there are a plethora of options available to a new company. The plan must specify what percentage of parts will be purchased, what percentage will be jobbed out, what percentage will be manufactured in-house, and where the final product will be assembled. These options create other problems which must be addressed, such as how quality will be controlled, how the company will avoid reliance on one manufacturer or jobbei for critical parts, and what the lead time for new sources will be. Since the initial production process will almost certainly change, the anticipated time frame for the change and format of the new production process should be identified.

Production costs need to be forecast. The production costs for various production levels, the anticipated floor space required and its cost, and the cost of capital equipment and its depreciable life should be identified. Much of this information may be unavailable. The purpose of this discussion is to persuade the venture capitalist of the entrepreneur's competence as well as to develop sophisticated financial forecasts. While a detailed cost breakdown is useful to investors, not all this information should be included in a business plan which will be widely distributed. Information should also be provided about how the company will finance inventories of both finished products and raw materials.

Financial Strategy and Projections

The amount of financial information necessary in a business plan depends on the stage of the company's development and on the amount of money being sought. The more advanced the company's development and the more funds the entrepreneur is seeking, the more detailed the discussion should be. In any event, the discussion of the company's financial requirements should begin with estimates of the quarterly expenditures projected for the next three to five years and the cumulative debt the company needs to retire immediately upon financing. The expected uses of this money should be detailed. A time line of financial events visually demonstrating expenditures is often helpful. Of the funds required, the amount which the company intends to finance through debt should be broken out.

Once the expenditures have been broken out, the company needs to show investors the potential returns from their investment. A profit and loss statement should be developed to demonstrate the company's potential profitability. The approximate price per share and the offering's timing are then combined with the returns per share and the return on investment. If future equity offerings are anticipated, the business plan should show the current investors' expected dilution of ownership. Most venture capitalists expect portfolio companies to have the potential to go public within five to seven years. Because going public is the venture capitalist's primary method of liquidating his investment, most venture capitalists will not invest in a company with no potential to go public. If the business plan indicates the company will not be large enough to go public (minimum sales: $20 million), or if management does not want to go public because it fears losing control, then few venture capitalists will consider the business plan.

Historic financial statements and projections for the next three to five years should be listed in tables in this section. Profit and loss statements should be broken out monthly until the company breaks even, and then should be projected on a semiannual basis for the remainder of the five year period. All key assumptions used in developing these statements should be listed. Every questionable assumption should be justified. If the assumptions are not listed and explained where necessary, then the venture capitalist will not believe the veracity of the financial data. Next to the market analysis, the most critical part of the business plan focuses on the cash flow. The flow of cash determines whether the enterprise will be a healthy one, an anemic one, or ultimately a dead one. Current cash flows as well as cash flow forecasts, by the month, by the week, by the day, tell an investor a great deal. A lot of companies can be profitable on an income-statement basis but are losing their shirts on a cash basis, and therefore will shortly be out of money and out of business. Emerging companies tend to forget the importance of cash flow. They think that if they sell a product and get it out the door, then they have done their job, and can move on to the next sale. But the entrepreneur must collect on that sale and get the money into his bank account to have money to pay the bills.

Summary

A one-page summary of the key strengths of the business plan can help emphasize its viability and leave the venture capitalist feeling positively about the company's potential. The summary should emphasize the potential benefits to the investor.

Appendixes

As appropriate, the business plan should include, in an appendix, information that was not necessary for the discussion in the general text, but which is useful to the investor for reference. Information in the appendixes should only be included if relevant or helpful. Appendixes may include the following:

1. biographies of key personnel, corporate directors, advisors, and consultants;
2. list of key assumptions;
3. list of all financial projections and data;
4. pictures and diagrams of the product or service;
5. professional references;
6. market studies and articles from trade journals; and
7. patents.

There are essentially three critical elements to the modern entrepreneurial effort: the development of a product or service or idea; the capital provided;

and the ability to market it. An effective business plan brings these elements together into a coherent and integrated picture of the company.

Suggested Readings

Outline for a New High Technology Business Plan, Arthur Young and Company, 1983.

Raising Venture Capital: An Entrepreneur's Guidebook, Deloitte Haskins & Sells, 1982.

Spohr, Anthony P. and Leslie Wat, *Forming R&D Partnerships,* Deloitte Haskins & Sells, 1983.

Wat, Leslie, *Strategies for Going Public,* Deloitte Haskins & Sells, 1983.

Selected Bibliography

"A Leveraged Buyout: What It Takes." *Business Week,* July 18, 1983, p. 194.

"Acquisitions of Venture-Backed Companies in 1982." *Venture Capital Journal,* December 1982, p. 5.

Berss, Marcia. "Geoff Taylor's Deep Pockets." *Forbes,* November 7, 1983, p. 62.

Briggs, Jean A. "We Need Entrepreneurs, Not Military Heroes." *Forbes,* November 7, 1983, p. 134.

Bylinski, Gene. *The Innovation Millionaires: How They Succeed.* New York: Scribner & Sons, 1976.

"Capital Transfusion for 1982—$1.4 Billion for 54 Venture Funds." *Venture Capital Journal,* January 1983, p. 6.

"Capital Transfusion 1982: More Than $700 Million for 33 Venture Funds." *Venture Capital Journal,* July 1983, p. 4.

Clark, Dave. "Vencap Southwest." *Financial Trend,* January–April 1984.

Clark, Dave. "Venture Capital for the Orphans." *Texas Business,* August 1984, p. 95.

"Corporate Financing in the 80's." *Venture,* June 1983, p. 65.

"Despite Greater Risks, More Banks Turn to Venture Capital Business." *Wall Street Journal,* November 28, 1983, p. 33.

Dizard, John W. "Europe Rediscovers the Entrepreneur." *Fortune,* October 3, 1983, p. 164.

Dobkin, Richard. "Evaluating a Proposed Merger: The Accounting Trouble Spots." *The Practical Accountant,* January 1982, p. 45.

Dominguez, John R. *Venture Capital.* Lexington, Massachusetts: Lexington Books, 1974.

Dorfman, Dan. "Venture Capital Game is Risky—And Profitable," *Austin American-Statesman,* February 20, 1984.

Eisenberg, Richard. "Venture Capital Made Easy." *USA Today,* February 22, 1984.

Emmett, Robert. "How to Value a Potential Acquisition." *Financial Executive,* February 1982, p. 16.

"Entrepreneurs Come of Age on the Continent." *Business Week,* December 12, 1983, p. 45.

Entrepreneurship: The Japanese Experience. Komiyama Printing Company, 1983.

"Executives Assess Europe's Technology Decline." *Wall Street Journal,* February 1, 1984, p. 28.

Gladstone, David. *Venture Capital Handbook: An Entrepreneur's Guide to Obtaining Capital to Start a Business, Buy a Business, or Grow an Existing Business.* Reston, Virginia: Reston Publishing Co., 1983.

"High-Tech Start-Up Firms to be Subsidized by MITI." *Japan Economic Journal,* February 14, 1984, p. 1.

Huey, John. "Executives Assess Europe's Technology Decline." *Wall Street Journal,* February 1, 1984, p. 28.

Inside R&D. February 1, 1984.

Jacobs, Stanford L. "Firms Seeking Venture Capital Must Weigh Strings Attached." *Wall Street Journal,* August 1, 1983, p. 29.

"Japan: Smoothing the Way for Venture Capital—Again." *Business Week,* October 11, 1982, p. 53.

"Japan Takes Plunge into Venture Funds." *Venture,* July 1982, p. 6.

Kiriyama, Masaru. "Bank of Tokyo's California Unit Sets Up Venture Capital." *Japan Economic Journal,* September 6, 1983, p. 1.

Kiyonari, Tadao. "Small Business Energizes the Japanese Economy." *Economic Eye,* December 1981, p. 24.

Kleschnick, Michael. *Venture Capital and Urban Development.* Washington, D.C.: Council of State Planning Agencies, 1979.

Kravitt, Gregory I. *How to Raise Capital: Preparing and Presenting a Business Plan.* Homewood, Ill.: Dow-Jones-Irwin, 1983.

"Laying Off R&D Risks on Tax Shelter Investors." *Business Week,* March 5, 1984, p. 80.

Levine, Jon. "Money for the Asking." *Venture,* June 1983, p. 34.

Levine, Jon. "Once Again, It's A Buyer's Market." *Venture,* June 1982, p. 80.

Lindorff, Dave. "The U.K.'s Three New Venture Funds." *Venture,* April 1982, p. 50.

Loftin, Richard. *Databook of Venture Capital Sources for High Technology Companies.* Washington, D.C.: Financial Data Corp, 1981.

Mancuso, Joseph. *How to Prepare and Present a Business Plan.* Englewood Cliffs, N.J.: Prentice-Hall, 1983.

Mills, Bradford. "The Leveraged Buy-Out." In *Guide to Venture Capital Sources,* Stanley M. Rubel, ed. Boston: Capital Publishing, 1974, p. 96.

Minard, Lawrence. "A Touch of Capitalism." *Forbes,* May 9, 1983, p. 118.

"More, But Later." *Forbes,* July 4, 1983, p. 147.

"More Risk Than Reward? A Hard Look at Publicly Owned Venture Capital Companies." *Barrons,* June 24, 1981, p. 4.

Murphy, Thomas P. "A Book I Almost Didn't Read." *Forbes,* March 28, 1983, p. 212.

Murphy, Thomas P. "Good-Bye SEC." *Forbes,* February 27, 1984, p. 200.

Murphy, Thomas P. "The Worm Turns." *Forbes,* January 1984, p. 210.

National Governor's Association. *Technology and Growth: State Initiatives in Technological Innovation* (draft). Final Report, Task Force on Technological Innovation, Committee on Transportation, Commerce and Technology.

"Paying a Premium for a Piece of the Action." *Business Week,* April 25, 1983, p. 116.

Pratt, Stanley E., ed. *Guide to Venture Capital Sources.* Wellesley Hills, Massachusetts: Capital Publishing Corp., 1982.

Roberts, Johnnie L. "After Rough Start, Venture Capital Firm Finds Success Backing Minority Businesses." *Wall Street Journal,* February 10, 1984, p. 33.

Roberts, Johnnie L. "Narragansett Managers Offer to Buy Concern." *Wall Street Journal,* January 23, 1984, p. 14.

Ross, Irwin. "How the Champs Do Leveraged Buyouts." *Fortune,* January 23, 1984, p. 70.

Silver, David A. *"Who's Who in Venture Capital."* New York: Competere Publishing Group, 1982.

Smith, Roger. "Doors Open for Venture Capital." *Sweden Now,* June 1983, p. 19.

Smith, William G. "Money, Money, Money." *Texas Business,* August 1983, p. 39.

"Software Development—A Venture Investment Trend." *Venture Capital Journal,* April 1983, p. 8.

"States Venturing Into Venture Capital—Opportunity or Problem?" *Venture Capital Journal,* September 1983, p. 7.

Tagliabue, John. "West German Venture Capital." *New York Times,* June 6, 1983, p. D7.

"The Big Money Paribas is Betting on Overseas Ventures." *Business Week,* December 12, 1983, p. 45.

"The Role of Venture Capital in the EEC." *European Trends,* January 1983, p. 34.

"Trends in Venture Investing, Part I." *Venture Capital Journal,* November 1982, p. 6.

"Trends in Venture Investing, Part II." *Venture Capital Journal,* December 1983, p. 4.

U.S. Department of Commerce, National Bureau of Standards. *Evaluating the Impact of Securities Regulation on Venture Capital Markets.* Prepared by James R. Barth. Washington, D.C.: Government Printing Office, 1980.

U.S. General Accounting Office. *Government–Industry Cooperation Can Enhance the Venture Capital Process.* GAO/AMD-82-35, August 12, 1982.

U.S. Small Business Administration. *SBIC Digest.* April 1982.

"Venture Capital Coast to Coast—Texas." *Venture Capital Journal,* February 1983, p. 4.

"Venture Capital Coast to Coast—Texas." *Venture Capital Journal,* August 1980, p. 7.

"Venture Capital Disbursements 1981: A Statistical Overview." *Venture Capital Journal,* June 1982, p. 7.

"Venture Capital Goes Continental." *Institutional Investor* (International Ed.), July 1983, p. 159.

"Venture Capital in Germany." *American Banker,* June 24, 1983, p. 13.

"Venture Capital in Japan: Scramble for Firms to Invest In." *The Oriental Economist,* November 1983, p. 8.

"Venture Capital in High Tech Acquisitions." *Mergers and Acquisitions,* Fall 1982, p. 40.

"Venture Capital: Money Chasing Innovation." *Computerworld,* May 23, 1983, p. 12.

"Venture Firms Proliferate; Sales Will Double in 3 Years." *Japan Economic Journal,* October 4, 1983, p. 1.

"Venture Investments in the Public Marketplace." *Venture Capital Journal,* March 1983, p. 7.

Vetter, Edward O. "Capital Venturing in Texas." Presentation to Technology Venturing Workshop, University of Texas at Arlington, November 28, 1983.

Walbert, Laura R. "Smart Money?" *Forbes,* May 7, 1981, p. 124.

Wallace, Anise C. "Magic Financing Via R&D Partnerships." *High Technology,* July 1983, p. 65.

Warren, Russell J. and Robert E. Kempenick. "Corporate Venturing: A Complement to Acquisition." *Mergers and Acquisitions,* Winter 1984, p. 65.

"Who's Who in Buyout Financing." *Venture,* August 1983, p. 102.

"You Should Know—Wharton's Own Venture." *Venture,* June 1983, p. 76.

Index

Index

About the Authors

George Kozmetsky is Executive Associate for Economic Affairs for the University of Texas System. In addition, he serves as Director of the IC² Institute of the University of Texas at Austin and holds the J. Marion West Chair Professorship. Dr. Kozmetsky is a professor of management and computer sciences at the University of Texas at Austin, and an adjunct professor in the Department of Medicine, University of Texas Health Science Center at San Antonio. From 1966 to 1982, he served as Dean of the College of Business Administration and the Graduate School of Business, University of Texas at Austin.

He entered the business world in 1952 at Hughes Aircraft Company. He later joined Litton Industries, rising to Vice-President and Assistant General Manager of the electronic equipment division. In 1960, Dr. Kozmetsky and a Litton associate founded Teledyne, Inc. He serves on several corporate boards among which are Datapoint Corporation, Heizer Corporation, La Quinta Motor Inns, Inc., MCO Holdings, Inc., MCO Resources, Inc., Teledyne, and Wrather Corporation.

Dr. Kozmetsky is a former president of the Institute of Management Sciences (TIMS) and a member of AAAS, AICPA, a fellow of the British Interplanetary Society, and chancellor of the American Society for Macro-Engineering.

A native of Seattle, Washington, Dr. Kozmetsky received the Bachelor of Arts degree from the University of Washington (1938), and the Master of Business Administration (1947) and Doctor of Commercial Science (1957) degrees from Harvard University. He has been a faculty member in the Harvard Business School and the Carnegie Institute of Technology (now Carnegie-Mellon University).

Michael Gill is the Assistant to the Chairman of the Board, MCO Resources, and a Research Fellow in the IC² Institute of the University of Texas at Austin. He has been an active researcher and writer on the venture industry for the past two years and has reviewed from an investor's viewpoint many venture capital proposals.

Mr. Gill has published through the IC² Institute a number of articles on venture capital and has been invited to speak on the subject to various groups. His research interests include technology commercialization, regional economic development, venture capital, high technology employment and financing, and investment in public issues of new technology stocks. He holds a B.A. in Economics and History from Villanova University and an M.B.A. from the University of Texas at Austin.

Raymond Smilor is the Associate Director of the IC² Institute at the University of Texas at Austin, and serves there as a member of the faculty in the Department of Marketing in the College of Business Administration. He also holds the Judson Neff Centennial Fellowship in the IC² Institute.

He has served as a research fellow for the National Science Foundation for an international exchange program on computers and management between the United States and the Soviet Union. He has been a leading participant in the planning and organization of many regional, national, and international conferences, symposia, and workshops, and serves as a consultant to business, government, and the non-profit sector. He is President of the Management Strategies Group and a Director of the Texas Lyceum Association. He appears in *Who's Who in the South and Southwest.*

Dr. Smilor's academic works have covered a wide variety of interdisciplinary subjects. He has taught courses on the graduate and undergraduate level in management, and currently teaches a course on "Marketing, Technology and Entrepreneurship." His research interests include science and technology transfer, regional economic analysis, marketing strategies for high technology products, and creative and innovative management techniques. He has edited or co-edited a number of books, the most recent of which is *Corporate Creativity: Robust Companies and the Entrepreneurial Spirit* (Praeger, 1984). Dr. Smilor earned his Ph.D. in U.S. History at the University of Texas at Austin.

About the IC² Institute

The IC² Institute at the University of Texas at Austin is a national center for the study of innovation, creativity, and capital. IC² studies are designed to develop alternatives for private sector action aimed at regional and national goals.

Some of the specific areas of research and study at IC² include the management of technology; creative and innovative management; the state of society; dynamic business development and entrepreneurship; new methods of economic analysis; and the determination of attitudes, concerns, and opinions on key issues.

The Institute also maintains a strong interaction between scholarly developments and real-world issues by conducting a variety of conferences. IC² research is published in a series of monographs, policy papers, research articles, and books.